Praise for Boy-stero

"I highly recommend this book to every woman who wants to understand boys."
— RICK JOHNSON, author of *That's My Son*

"Jean Blackmer understands boys! In her uniquely personal, humorous, and insightful style, she tells parents of boys what they need to know."
— CAROL KUYKENDALL, speaker and author of *Five Simple Ways to Grow a Great Family*

"Jean has done a great service to moms everywhere by encouraging them to enjoy the wild and wonderful journey of rearing a son."
— DR. KEVIN LEMAN, author of *Have a New Kid by Friday*

"Life with boys is part mystery, part comedy, and all adventure! Jean Blackmer equips parents to understand the mystery, laugh at the comedy, and buckle in for the adventure. Enjoy!"
— CARLA FOOTE, director of media and executive editor of *MomSense Magazine*, MOPS International

BOY-STEROUS LIVING

celebrating your loud and rowdy life with sons

Jean Blackmer

BEACON HILL PRESS
OF KANSAS CITY

Library of Congress Cataloging-in-Publication Data
Blackmer, Jean, 1964-
   Boy-sterous living : celebrating your loud and rowdy life with sons /
Jean Blackmer.
      p. cm.
   Includes bibliographical references (p.   ).
   ISBN 978-0-8341-2390-8 (pbk.)
   1. Mothers and sons—Religious aspects—Christianity. 2. Parenting—
Religious aspects—Christianity. 3. Sons—Religious life. I. Title.
   BV4529.18.B476 2008
   248.8'431—dc22
                                                    2008028765

10 9 8 7 6 5 4 3 2 1

Boy: a noise with dirt on it.
—Aidan Miller,
Not Your Average Dictionary Homelife Edition

Contents

Acknowledgments

To my husband, and my three boys, Josh, Jordan, and Jake: You are awesome! Thanks for loving me and allowing me to share some of our family stories. You make great book material. I'm grateful to God most of all for making us a family.

Thanks to my sisters, Leslie and Jill and their families, and to Mimi and Papa. Your influence in our family began from the very beginning. And thanks to my many friends who allowed me to share some of their boy experiences.

Thanks to my Bible study group: without you, I don't know what I would do.

A special thanks goes to Kirsten Otey, mom of three boys: you have a great sense of humor, and you're one of the most brilliant editors ever.

And thank you Bonnie Perry and Judi Perry and the team at Beacon Hill Press of Kansas City for embracing my vision and printing this book.

May all parents of boys find joy and encouragement as they live a full, loud, life.

Introduction

I really don't understand why boys like loud noises. I have three boys, Josh, Jordan, and Jake, and a day doesn't go by that I don't ask them to turn down the volume on something. I'm always turning down the TV set, the stereo, and the computer speakers. I used to think one of them had poor hearing—but *all* of them? Something is definitely going on in their brains that isn't going on in mine. And boys don't seem to outgrow it. Even my husband, Zane, loves loud noises. We're always in battle with each other for the control knob on the car stereo—I'm trying to turn it down while he's trying to turn it up.

On one of our road trips from Colorado to Utah, the boys noticed that the louder the stereo, the faster Daddy drove. Against my protests, they kept encouraging him to turn it up. At one point I looked at the speedometer and realized Zane was driving about 90 miles per hour. The stereo was blaring, and the boys were laughing in the back seat. I finally figured out their plot was to get Daddy to drive fast in order to arrive at our destination ASAP.

To me, this is proof that loud noises have a stimulating effect on boys, with or without their knowledge. It's sort of like drinking a caffeine-laden soda, which boys should never be allowed to have—loud noises energize them. It's like an addiction that gets their adrenaline going.

I'm convinced that this is the reason the boys keep a large brown paper bag filled with noisy fireworks in our bedroom closet. They pull the bag out for New Year's, birthdays, Presidents' Day—just about any celebration, including our wedding anniversary. And they love it!

I dread it.

I worry about what our neighbors will think when the boys set off the fireworks, which is usually when it's extremely dark and quiet outside. I stand nearby with a broom, a dustpan, and a trash bag so they can clean up the evidence that all that noise was coming from our house. I doubt I'm fooling anyone—we're the only family on the block with three boys. We live in a neighborhood of wonderful, quiet, elderly folks, who happen to like their sleep and tend to worry about loud explosions in the middle of the night.

For the most part, I think our neighbors have grown accustomed to us. They often make a point of stopping by to tell me how much they enjoy hearing kid noises in the neighborhood, because it keeps them feeling young and reminds them of when their own children were growing up. I try to believe it.

Nothing seems to surprise my neighbors—even when something surprises me. One sunny Saturday I drove up to find sheer chaos in our front yard. Even the neighborhood men had gathered to watch the spectacle.

A friend had given Zane a tape of squawking crows. Zane wants me to let you know the tape can be purchased at Cabella's for only $9.95, in case you're looking for the perfect gift for your hubby. I would not recommend it, however.

The purpose of the tape? To attract crows to your yard, of course. I had no idea why anyone would want to do that, but I was about to find out.

Hordes of black crows had eerily appeared. Hundreds of them were gathered in the big maple tree in the front yard. And more black shadows circled above, squawking and searching for a place to land. It reminded me of a scene from Alfred Hitchcock's horror movie *The Birds*. I jumped out of my minivan and sprinted into the house.

Not only was the sound of the tape coming full blast through the front door, but the visiting birds were joining in with their own earsplitting cackles. Our chocolate lab, Toby, was going berserk, barking furiously and running through the house trying to get outside. The noise was unbelievable. I covered my ears and yelled, "What's going on?"

"Hi, Honey!" Zane hollered as he rushed out the front door trying to catch Toby, who dashed out as I dashed in.

The boys were laughing so hard that they never heard me or noticed I was home.

Zane returned, dragging Toby by his collar, and locked him in the bathroom, where he continued to bark. Then Zane ran into the kitchen.

"What are you doing?" I yelled again.

"Getting the BB gun." He kept it hidden in the pantry.

"What? Are you crazy?" I asked.

He looked at me as if *I* were crazy. "That's what the tape is for—shooting practice."

I put my foot down when I heard that. No way did I want Zane, the boys, and all the neighborhood men shooting at the innocent birds who were tricked into coming to our tree. Besides, we live in the city limits; it's illegal to shoot animals, even if it's just to startle them. I turned off the tape player. The dog quickly quit barking, the birds slowly left the tree, and the neighbors drifted out of the yard. The boys were mad at me for ruining their fun.

I felt a little guilty for it, but I honestly didn't understand what there was about this that could be fun.

I'm a girl. I constantly have to remind them of that fact. They're boys, which needs no reminder. We're wired differently. I don't like loud noises, and they love them. I don't drive faster with loud music, and noise does not energize me. In fact, noise gives me a headache. But I didn't want to completely squelch their fun. Compromise seemed like a good, well—compromise.

So we sat down at the table, and I said, "Okay. We can play the tape, but no shooting at the innocent—" Before I could even finish my sentence, the tape was back on, the dog was barking, and Zane and the boys were running around the house looking for the BB gun, which I had hidden. *So much for compromise, or listening skills, for that matter,* I thought as I covered my ears and went in search of aspirin.

This is a fact: life with boys is loud. If it's quiet, they're probably up to something they shouldn't be doing and don't want you to know about. Rather than fight this fact, I've learned to accept it and have even come to believe *loud* is not necessarily bad. After 20 years of living with boys, living loud means, to me, not only living with lots of noise but also living life with passion, humor, adventure, and endless energy. As I've interviewed other parents of boys for this book, I've found they feel the same way. And, like me, they love their boys, love to laugh, need their friends, and most important, seek guidance from God to help them on their journey of raising tomorrow's men.

In this book you'll read many "parents of boys" stories— stories that will make you smile and even laugh out loud. Life with boys means no dull moments. So, I hope, does reading this book.

After each chapter is a section containing thought-provoking questions, practical tips, interesting facts and statistics, and Bible verses to apply to your life.

My prayer is that you'll find your life with boys to be a life full of passion, humor, and adventure. And may God grant you the endless energy required to keep up with your boys.

Cheers to living *boy-sterously!*

Jean

1. Choose to Laugh

Our mouths were filled with laughter, our tongues with songs of joy.
Then it was said among the nations, "The LORD has done
great things for them." The LORD has done
great things for us, and we are filled with joy.
—Psalm 126:2-3.

Just when I thought my youngest son, Jake, was old enough to take a shower without constant supervision, he did something that shocked me. He got out of the shower, dried off and dressed, and stood in front of me looking as if he wanted to tell me something. I looked at him for a moment, asking myself, *Why does he look so different?*

Then it hit me.

"Jake, did you shave off your eyebrows?" I asked.

"Yep," he said. I think he was waiting to see me go through the roof.

"Um—why?" I asked.

"I watch Daddy shave, and I wanted to try it. That was the only hair on my face."

His eyebrows were completely gone! He had cleanly shaven them off. Fortunately, he hadn't cut himself. I had mixed emotions as I looked at him standing so innocently in the kitchen. I knew he was imitating his father, and that's a normal thing for a boy, but I never dreamed he would take a razor and carefully shave off his eyebrows. I wanted to scold him—he knew better than to play with a razor. At the same time, I felt an uncontrollable urge to laugh. What else could I do? I exploded with laughter. He started laughing, too—I think from relief that I didn't lecture him or ground him or make him scrub the bathroom floor with a toothbrush.

"Wow, that looks so—weird," I said as I ran my thumb over his eye where his eyebrow once was.

He started laughing even harder. "How long do you think it will take to grow them back?" He barely got his question out between giggles.

"I have no idea." That was my standard answer for most of my boys' questions.

It took a long time—like until Christmas, which turned out okay because we came up with a unique Christmas card that year.

I love getting cards from friends and families around the country, but sometimes they seem sort of, well—superficial. For some reason people decide that's a good time to update everyone on their past year's accomplishments, including but not limited to, their kids' activities, ranging from ballet to football to fencing, their kids' academic excellence, new pets, world travels, and any other topics of interest or disinterest to their readers. I know many people put many hours into writing those heartfelt Christmas letters, but what about those of us who have nothing to say except "My son shaved off his eyebrows this past year"?

So instead of trying to create a long letter to make our life sound better than it actually is, we did a different type of Christmas greeting. A picture was definitely out of the question since Jake still looked kind of weird. So we sent out a one-pager, titled at the top, "What I Learned About Life Last Year." Then each person in our family wrote a quick sentence about something he or she had learned. But it had to be something silly—nothing serious or deep. We were going for goofy but true. We wrote the following:

> *I learned to never hug your dog when he comes running to you unexpectedly. Mine had just been sprayed by a skunk, and it took days for the smell to leave my hair and pajamas.* **—Jean**
>
> *I learned to never hug your wife after she's hugged the dog that was just sprayed by a skunk. And it's not a good idea to make her take off her skunk-smelling pajamas on the front porch and leave them in the yard for three days. The neighbors are still wondering about that.*
> *P.S. Tomato juice does not get rid of skunk smell.* **—Zane**
>
> *I learned never to let my mom cut my hair ever again. The bald patches were really embarrassing, and I had to wear a baseball cap for five weeks.* **—Josh**
>
> *I learned never to make your little brother mad; it can be dangerous.* **—Jordan**
>
> *I learned never to shave off your eyebrows. They take a really long time to grow back.* **—Jake**

We had fun writing these and getting responses back. We received notes from families with funny little stories about their children and their lives, and these notes kept us laughing all season long.

From this experience, I realized people really do love to laugh, and funny stories spark memories of someone's own funny stories. Then they get passed around, creating joyful memories for many families.

I know life is not always funny. It's not funny when your teenage daughter is cutting herself or when your son is addicted to drugs and then steals your money to fund his habit and you have to send him away to a special treatment program. Those things will make you cry, and cry hard.

Sometimes laughing hurts someone else's feelings. Boys love to spar verbally with each other. And being boys, they try not to show that words truly do hurt. The saying "Sticks and stones may break my bones, but words will never harm me" is a bunch of baloney. Sometimes family members tease each other to tears. In his book *Good Spousekeeping*, Dave Meurer offers a great guideline for joking with each other: "If only one of you thinks something is funny, it isn't."[1]

I don't know how anyone gets through life without a daily dose of laughter, especially when raising sons. If I took everything seriously, I would probably lose my mind. Laughter is a great stress-reliever, and anyone rearing a son knows how stressful that can be. Sometimes my boys will do something that completely throws me for a loop—something so unexpected and so ridiculous, like shaving off their eyebrows, that all I can do is laugh. The other alternative is to scream and cry and stomp my feet, but where would that get me?

The writer of the Book of Proverbs must have been thinking of parents of boys, especially mothers, when he wrote, "She is clothed with strength and dignity; she can laugh at the days to come" (Proverbs 31:25). I guarantee that boys will give us plenty of things to laugh about in the days, months, and years to come. And like the Proverbs 31 woman, if we learn to laugh rather than scream, cry, and stomp our feet, we'll exhibit strength and dignity.

Laughter is a gracious gift from God. It's good medicine, especially in those moments of raising boys when we don't know whether to laugh or cry. Choose to laugh.

And never assume boys are old enough to be left alone with scissors, razors, or other sharp objects.

Digging Deeper

Did you know laughing is good for your health? It's widely believed that it reduces stress, lowers blood pressure, elevates mood, boosts the immune system, improves brain functioning, protects the heart, connects you to others, and fosters instant relaxation.

Unfortunately, most adults don't laugh as much as they did when they were children. An article entitled "Science of Laughter" on the Discovery Health Web site states, "By the time a child reaches nursery school, he or she will laugh about 300 times a day. Adults laugh an average of 12 times a day."[2]

This study also found that women laugh 126 percent more than men.

Questions for Reflection

How often do you laugh?

When was the last time you laughed?

Write down a funny story about your son, and read it to him. Children love to hear stories about themselves and will probably ask to hear it again and again.

How can you teach your boys the difference between laughing *with* someone and laughing *at* someone?

Plan a party with your friends, and ask everyone to share something funny his or child child did or said recently.

Suggested Reading

All *Calvin and Hobbes* comic books, by Bill Watterson.

Here are Scripture references for further insight regarding joy and laughter: Nehemiah 8:10; Psalm 81:1; Proverbs 17:22; Galatians 5:22.

2. The Fear Factor

Be strong and courageous. Do not be terrified; do not be discouraged,
*for the L*ORD *your God will be with you wherever you go.*
—Joshua 1:9

Boys and risk-taking go together like steak and potatoes. Boys' parents fear for their son's safety at some time or another. Whether the son is jumping off a roof into a swimming pool, biking down mountains at high speeds, playing a rough game of football, or long-boarding down steep hills, parents of boys *always* find something to fear.

Unfortunately, I'm a worrier, and living with three boys hasn't helped me with this problem. When the boys are late getting home, I fear there's been a car accident, a kidnapping, or that the late child has been eaten by a mountain lion. I don't know why I let my imagination get away from me in these situations, but the more imagining I do, the worse the scenarios become. It's a constant brain battle.

On weekends during the winter, my family goes skiing. The boys are old enough to explore the mountain on their own, yet every time I watch them leave, I worry that they might get knocked out somewhere in the trees, fall off the chairlift, tear a knee ligament, or break both thumbs in a bad fall.

And they do.

In just one season Josh fractured his lower leg while landing a front flip off a cliff. He spent three weeks recovering. Then during spring break he broke his collarbone during a jump in the terrain park. He wasn't even doing anything crazy—it was lousy snow and a lousy landing.

Jordan escaped serious injury when a careless snowboarder crashed into him. He was smart enough to place his metal ski pole between himself and the skier soaring toward him. Thankfully, the only damage done was a broken pole and a bruised snowboarder.

That same season, Jake discovered his love for skiing through the trees. I believe the angels I asked to guard him were kept very busy, because he survived with a few scrapes but nothing serious.

My husband, Zane, struggles with worrying about the boys too. He recently had a dream that he was sitting on a swing with Jake on his lap. Underneath them was a sleeping lion. Suddenly, the lion woke up and snatched Jake out of his hands. Zane tried desperately to rescue Jake, but his attempts failed. He woke up panicked and unable to sleep the rest of the night. One of his worst nightmares is to be in a dangerous situation where he is unable to protect the boys or me. Trusting God to take care of us is difficult for him and something he's learned to do over the years. But his fears still sometimes seep into his sleep.

I suspect Zane harbors some fears because he was a boy

himself, and he remembers how he was and thus knows—even more than I—all there is to worry about. He did so many insane things as a child that he's truly thankful he survived his childhood. And he hopes his boys will be smarter than he was while he was growing up.

Neither of us wants to fret and fear, and I'm sure other parents don't either. So how do we keep from feeling afraid as we watch our boys go out the door each day?

I gained some insight from a mom I was fortunate to meet when I flew to California to interview Michael, a young man with a miraculous story of survival in the wilderness. Michael, his dad, his uncle, and his cousin were stranded for almost a week during a brutal storm that dumped five feet of snow in the Sierra Nevada Mountains. (*Guideposts*, October 2007.)

After the interview with Michael, I couldn't stop wondering how his mom, Sue, felt during all of this. How did she handle her fear? So I interviewed her as well. This is Sue's story:

The savory smell of beef, onions, tomatoes, and garlic filled the kitchen. Sue stirred the thick stew with a wooden spoon and thought, Paul and Michael are gonna love this. After tasting a bit of it left on the spoon, she added a dash more salt. *They should be home any minute now.*

Actually, they should have been home hours ago. She looked out the window; the rain was coming down steadily now. *They'll sure be cold. This stew will warm them up.*

Sue's husband, Paul, and her 18-year-old son, Michael, had gone on a father-son getaway with her brother-in-law, Frank, and his 16-year-old son, Dominic. Their plan was to spend the weekend hiking and backpacking in the Sierra Nevada Mountains at an alpine spot called Rae Lake.

As Sue stirred the thick broth, the phone rang.

"Hey, Sue." It was her sister-in law, Mary. "Have you heard from the boys yet?"

"Not yet, I've tried calling both Paul and Michael's cell phones. No answer."

"They should have been home by now. Do you think they're all right?"

"Oh, I'm sure they're just fine. Probably having so much fun they don't want the weekend to end."

"I'm getting a little worried. Frank usually sticks to his plan and is never late. Dominic has school tomorrow, and I heard it's snowing up in the mountains." Mary's strained voice caused Sue's heartbeat to quicken. "Do you think we should call someone and report them missing?" Mary asked.

"Not yet. Why don't I come on over to your house, and we'll wait for them together. Then we can decide what to do."

As the hours wore on, the two women's worries increased. At 10 P.M. they decided to report the group missing. Sue made the phone call. "They're gonna kill us when they find out we sent out a search party," she said to Mary.

"Yeah, maybe we're overreacting. Let's call back and tell the operator to cancel the report," Mary suggested. But it was too late. The irritated operator informed them that the search had begun.

The next morning the boys still hadn't returned. Sue couldn't help but worry that something horrible had happened. She imagined their car tumbling over the edge of the road into the river or Michael wandering off on his own and getting lost. Sue decided to stay at Mary's house. She couldn't stand being in her home without the boys, and her daughter, Stephanie, was at college.

Finally the phone rang. "We found their car," the sheriff said, "at the Rae Lake Trailhead, which means they're still up there somewhere. We'll find them, don't worry. We always find who we're looking for."

At least they know where they are. But as Sue thought about what the sheriff had said, dread filled her. Actually, it's what he *didn't* say that upset her. *Dead or alive, they* always *find the person.* She held back her tears and tried to hold on to hope.

The hours gradually turned into days of waiting, worrying, and waiting some more. Stephanie came home to be with her and wait. The gray skies kept releasing their wrath of rain and snow, never letting up.

Meanwhile, the rescuers were risking their own lives to find the boys. The deep, wet snow made it impossible for snowmobiles or horses, so they headed out on snowshoes. Ten men, known as ground pounders, carrying 60-pound packs, set out on the trail to find Sue's missing loved ones. It took them 24 hours to hike nine miles in the blustery conditions. They finally reached Fleming Lake, about a half-mile from Rae Lake, but that night a fierce wind kicked up, blowing away their tarps—their only shelter from the frigid wind and cold. They were also nearing the end of their supplies. They had to make a difficult decision.

The phone rang with the bad news. "I'm sorry Ma'am. We had to turn around," one of the rescuers told her. Hot tears leaked down Sue's cheeks as he spoke, and her stomach flip-flopped with fear.

The snow in the mountains was now about four feet deep and still piling up. The chance of reaching them on foot was now impossible. The rescuers had to wait for a break in the storm and then send a helicopter to find them. Who knew how long that would be?

Sue decided to go home and grab a couple of items belonging to Paul and Michael to keep close and comfort her. She grabbed Paul's wedding ring he'd left behind and placed it on her thumb. Then she went into Michael's room and noticed his Bible next to his bed. She picked up it and hugged it to her heart and prayed for their safety. Michael had just recently become a Christian and given up partying for Bible studies. Then she opened it and began flipping through the pages. *Michael held this a few days ago. I wonder what he read, what he thought, what he prayed.*

Then she noticed a few verses underlined: "Be strong and courageous. Do not be terrified; do not be discouraged, for the LORD your God will be with you wherever you go" (Joshua 1:9).

Lord, she prayed, *Michael just read these verses. I pray he and Paul will be strong and courageous right now wherever they are, and I trust you are with them.* She began praying that verse over and over again throughout the seemingly endless days of waiting. Each night Stephanie read those verses out loud and prayed, causing Sue to weep some more, yet Sue clung to the hope those verses offered.

Sue had barely slept for four and a half days. She didn't know if the boys were dead or alive. Each day drained her of hope for their survival, especially as the snow continued to fall. Others tried to encourage her. The house was constantly full of caring family, neighbors, friends, and even media people. The whole town was waiting to hear about the four beloved men who were missing. People put ribbons around trees, hung banners on the high school, and continually dropped encouraging notes, food, and gifts at Mary's home. But the deep-seeded knot of fear threatened to choke out her hope. She continued to pray for them.

Almost five days after the boys had left on their trip, the sinister-looking clouds disappeared. Sunshine brightened the blue sky. Finally they could send the helicopter.

"The chopper is in the air," a sheriff's deputy reported to an exhausted Sue. About an hour later the phone rang again. Sue raced to answer it, and the room full of visitors became silent.

"We found them—they're all okay!" the sheriff shouted over the roar of the helicopter rotors.

Sue's knees buckled under her. "They're all okay," she whispered to Mary as she knelt on the kitchen floor. Stephanie ran to her mom, and they shared a hug and a flood of tears. The silent room erupted into cheering, crying, hugging, and cameras flashing. The boys were safe.

After being examined at a hospital, they were all able to come home. Paul and Sue hugged long as he cried on her shoulder. Then she saw Michael, her son. He had a scruffy beard, messy hair, and dark circles under his eyes, but he carried himself with pride. He hugged Sue, and she searched his teary eyes and saw, perhaps for the first time, the face of a man—a wise, strong man who could survive whatever life threw at him.

Later that night, as they finally ate the stew she had made, she told Michael about the verses she had found underlined in his Bible, the ones she and Stephanie read each night. "I thought about those words constantly," he said. "That's one of the only verses I've memorized." They both started crying and hugged again.

Michael was comforted to know God had given Sue those verses to pray for him, the exact ones on his heart. And Sue was comforted to know that her son was strong and courageous and that God was, and is, with him wherever he may go.

After talking with Sue, I knew to expect times of feeling

afraid for my boys and their safety. They'll be in dangerous situations. Fear is inevitable, but giving into fear is *my* choice. Sue showed me that I can let my mind wander and dream up all sorts of horrible situations, or I can turn off that part of my brain and think about what's true. I can pray and trust that God is with my boys wherever they go.

My friend Kirsten, a mother of three boys, shared a story with me about her middle son, Travis. Travis is the type of kid who believes that if something is in his path, it needs to be jumped or climbed. For example, rather than walking down porch steps, he prefers jumping over the railing. According to Kirsten, he's very confident, exhibits no fear, and exercises no caution. He's been like this since he was a baby. I know, because I used to take care of him while Kirsten attended classes for her Ph.D. I'll never forget when he rolled off the changing table as I looked away for just a moment to reach for a baby wipe. I watched him fall and hit the carpeted floor. I was horrified and waited for him to start screaming. Instead, he looked at me and smiled, as though he thought it was kind of fun.

When Travis was 10 years old, their family visited Washington, D.C. After brunch at the Smithsonian Castle building, they walked in the drizzling rain across an overpass to where their car was parked. Alongside the sidewalk was a waist-high, two-foot-wide, rounded cement railing. Travis immediately jumped up on it and started skip-walking. Kirsten looked over the edge and to her horror saw a 50-foot drop to train tracks and a road below. As any parent would, she freaked out and demanded he get down immediately.

Over the next few years, Kirsten periodically relived the experience in her mind, except that she would imagine Travis plummeting to his death. Sometimes at night the scene would keep her awake as she tossed and turned. Sometimes during the day she obsessed about it until her heart raced. Finally she began pleading with God to erase the memory so she could have peace. When God answered her, though, He told her that He did not want her to forget the scene but to view it differently. As she prayed, she felt God gently whisper: *Kirsten, I was there with Travis, making sure that he did not fall. I care more about him than you do. I'm holding him. You can't think of everything and protect him from everything. You won't always be there, but I am.*

Kirsten felt a physical sense of peace as she accepted this as truth. She realized she can't always be there to protect Travis, and, like Sue, she had to reach a moment of trusting God and knowing He is with Travis wherever he goes.

Fearlessness Versus Foolishness

Another suggestion to help decrease fear is to teach boys to know the difference between *fearless* and *foolish*.

Fearless is defined at Dictionary.com as "bold, brave, possessing or exhibiting courage or courageous endurance."

Foolish is defined as "showing a lack of sense; ill-considered; unwise, lacking forethought."

Michael and his dad, uncle, and cousin were not foolish about planning their getaway. They had double-checked weather forecasts, packed the necessary equipment to camp for several days, and informed others about their destination. But the storm arrived early and was more severe than they expected. Suddenly they were fighting to stay alive. They had to live with courageous endurance. They rationed their food, sometimes eating watery oatmeal for breakfast, two peanuts for lunch, and a spoonful of peanut butter for dinner. They melted snow to drink. They read out loud to each other to pass the time, and they prayed together often. They zipped their sleeping bags together for added warmth and shared a pair of wool socks and a wool hat. This experience tested their strength, faith, and courage and ultimately brought them closer together as fathers and sons. They were fearless under those extreme conditions. They knew what to do, they did it, and they survived to tell others about it.

Hopefully, most parents of boys won't have to endure what Sue endured. But we do need to prepare our boys to face fear and live courageously, to be brave in the face of adversity. Training boys to be fearless when fearlessness is needed, but never foolish, is a challenge. Boys' brains don't usually operate in the realm of carefully considering the consequences of their actions.

Boys often tend to be spontaneous, having an attitude of "Just do it! Then whatever happens—happens!" This can be considered foolish, but as parents of boys, we can take these situations, especially when our boys are young, and turn them into learning opportunities to help them make better decisions in the future.

Some may disagree, but I think it's good to let boys live a little dangerously, as long as they aren't likely to seriously hurt themselves or someone else. If we always try to protect our boys to try to keep them safe, they may not develop the self-confidence and bravery they'll need later in life.

Trust your boys. Trust what you've taught them. Most of all, trust God. He's always with them.

Never stop praying for their safety. When the boys go skiing, I still pray they won't break both thumbs—and so far they haven't.

Digging Deeper

Read the story of David and Goliath found in 1 Samuel 17 aloud with your family, and discuss the following question: Do you think David was fearless or foolish? Why?

If you could teach your son(s) one survival skill, what would it be, and why?

What's your greatest fear about your son(s)? What can you do to decrease the fear you feel?

Plan an adventure with you son(s). As you plan, emphasize safety, but allow for a great adventure. Be creative. Maybe hike to a secluded lake to camp and fish, plan a paintball outing, mountain bike over a mountain, or camp on a beach.

Suggested Reading

Here are verses to read when you're feeling afraid: Psalm 23:4; Psalm 46:1-3; Psalm 94:19; Isaiah 41:10; Isaiah 41:13; 2 Timothy 1:7.

3. Communicating with the Caveman

When words are many, sin is not absent,
but he who holds his tongue is wise.
—Proverbs 10:8

Just this morning as I was preparing to write this chapter on communication, I experienced a real-life episode in our home that highlighted the differences in the ways males and females communicate.

Josh, who leaves the house at 6:50 A.M. to get a good parking space at his high school, strolled into the kitchen for breakfast. He plopped down on the stool at the kitchen island.

"Hi, Sweetie. How'd you sleep?" I asked, eager to talk with someone. I had already been up for a while and had my cup of coffee.

"Huh?"

"How—did—you—sleep?" I asked slowly.

"Good."

"Great. So, how's math going?"

"Fine."

"Hey, did you get back the calculator you loaned to your friend?"

"What?"

"Did—you—get—back—"

"Mom, just stop asking so many questions," he said as he put his sleepy head down onto the granite countertop.

Okay—he had a good point. Although my feelings were a little hurt, I realized I had asked too many questions, and it was too early in the day to be interrogated. I hugged him good-bye and told him to have a great day. He nodded as he grabbed a red plastic cup filled with some of the protein shake I had made and headed out the door.

Soon the other two boys meandered downstairs. Jake sat on the same stool as Josh, Jordan next to him.

"Hi, guys," I smiled, "How'd you sleep?"

"What?" they said simultaneously.

Here we go again. "How—did—you—sleep?"

"Good," they said, answering in unison.

Then Jordan disappeared into the pantry to search for cereal.

As I cleaned up the mess from making the protein shake, I tried to engage Jake in conversation without asking questions.

"So, you have football practice today after school."

"Yep."

"It's Friday. Don't forget to turn your current event paper in. I saw your math book up in your room, in case you need to take it today. Your cleats are behind your bedroom door."

"Huh?"

His face told me I'd overloaded him with information.

"Never mind," I said and continued wiping off the counter.

"Sorry, Mom. I completely zoned out. I didn't hear a word you said. You talk too much in the morning."

I remembered something a friend shared with me recently. Her six-year-old son had been playing for several hours with a little girl about the same age when suddenly he blurted out, "I'll pay you two dollars out of my piggy bank if you'll just stop talking!"

I responded to Jake, "Okay—how about you pay me two dollars a day, and I'll just stop talking?"

"What?" Jake asked.

"Oh, forget it."

"Forget what?" Jordan asked as he emerged from the pantry empty-handed.

"I was reminding Jake not to forget his math book."

"Huh?" Jordan stared blankly at me. Then he added, "I forgot what I was looking for."

"Cereal." I shook my head in disbelief.

So that's a glimpse into a usual morning in the Blackmer household: a talkative, caffeine-filled mom trying to communicate and connect with three boys.

After the boys left for school, Zane, who had left early to meet some of his buddies at a coffee shop, came home. I assailed him with questions.

"How's Jeff?" I asked.

"Fine," Zane answered as he sat down at the table and opened the newspaper.

"How's his new job?"

"Good."

"Did Joe come?"

"Nope."

"Did you get a latte?"

"Yep."

By this time I had had it. "Did you use up all your words for the day talking with your friends?" I snapped.

"What?" he asked.

Zane didn't know it, but I had spent a couple hours the day before researching communication differences between men and women—such as the number of words each gender uses per day. I found a variety of numbers, but everything I read agreed that, on any given day, women talk more than men.

But it was only 8:30 A.M. Surely Zane hadn't depleted his total word count. I just wanted to know a little more about his time with his friends.

"Did you plan your bike trip for next week?"

"Uh, I forgot."

"Did Jeff say how Tyler's birthday went?"

"No."

"Did they find their missing cat?"

"I don't know."

"Zane, why do I feel like I'm playing '20 questions' with you? Can't you just tell me stuff without my dragging the details out of you?"

"Oh, sorry, Honey. What do you want to know?" He put the paper down and looked me in the eyes. Fortunately, Zane is a good communicator when he focuses on it.

"Never mind. I've got to get to work on writing a chapter for my book. I don't have time to talk right now." I retreated to my writing loft to write about communicating with males.

It never fails. God tests you when you're in the midst of learning about something. And I think God showed me something surprising. As I searched the Bible for relevant scripture on the topic of communication, I didn't find any that said, "God loves a good talker." Instead, I noticed a recurring theme in the Bible, especially in the Book of Proverbs: people who talk too much are fools, and people who use restraint with words are wise. To me, this means my home is filled with very wise men, and I should value their ability to refrain from speaking excessively.

However, communicating with other human beings is a necessary life skill. I don't mean we should *force* boys to talk about everything all the time, but I do believe we need to encourage them to speak in full sentences, to use eye contact, to be quick to listen, and to be comfortable expressing their feelings.

Following are a few tips to encourage boys in the art of communication while keeping in mind that it's okay for boys to not be chatterboxes.

Timing Is Everything

Most boys, though not all of them, communicate using a variety of grunts, groans, and nods, especially in the morning. When my boys come down to the kitchen after a good night's sleep, they encounter me, a talkative female seeking meaningful conversation. At this time of day, they can barely open their eyes wide enough to find the cereal they want, if they even remember what they were looking for in the pantry.

Because I've ruled out mornings as a meaningful talking time, and the boys are now gone most of the day, are tired and hungry when they get home, and then have homework to do, I've found bedtime to be one of the best times to converse—which is unfortunate for me. By that time, I'm ready to fall into bed with a good book. I have little energy for interaction. I don't know if they're just trying to prolong going to bed, but it really doesn't matter. If the lights are out and they start talking, I'll try to engage, at least for a little while, even if that means going to bed a little later.

My boys are also "chattier" if we're doing something together, like hiking, skiing, or raking leaves. Other parents I spoke with agreed. One dad told me his son starts talking when they start shooting hoops. A mom told me a story about her son who loves to fish. When he was young, she often took him fishing, and they would talk. Her son is now an adult, and they have continued this ritual. Recently, he knocked on her door at 3 A.M. and told her he wanted to go fishing. She knew that meant he had something on his mind he wanted to talk about. She slipped on some warm clothes and grabbed her fishing pole. Oops—my husband chastises me for calling it a fishing *pole*. It's a fishing *rod*. Anyway, they spent the wee hours of the morning fishing and talking about his troubled marriage. Until the sun peeked over the horizon, he poured out his heart to her as they reeled in fish from the glassy pond dimly lit by the moon. Fishing together created an atmosphere in which he felt comfortable talking, and his wise mom understood that's what he needed in order to unlock his thoughts and discuss his life.

Another friend of mine, Rick Hamlin, executive editor

for *Guideposts* magazine and the dad of two boys aged 17 and 20, feels dinnertime is one of the best times for families to connect and communicate. "We always had the boys say grace before dinner. In their prayer, they usually mentioned things they were thankful for. That gave us a glimpse into their day and what was important to them." He also feels dinnertime conversations offer opportunities for parents to model how to interact with each other. "I think it's very important for parents to show emotional support for each other, to ask questions of each other, and to share stories about the day."

Many experts agree that sharing dinner together is a key ingredient to creating connectedness among family members. Author and speaker Carol Kuykendall writes in her book *Five Star Families: Moving Yours from Good to Great* that dinnertime was their family time. "It wasn't always easy, and it wasn't always pleasant with spilled milk and picky eaters and far too many conversations about bodily functions—complete with sounds effects. But dinner marked a special spot in the day, kind of like the comma between afternoon and evening. It was the one time of day when plural became singular. We said grace together. We passed the salt. We shared feelings and failures and funny stuff."[1]

Creating space for that "comma"—dinnertime—in your day, even if you have to listen to unpleasant sound effects, is a tradition worth keeping.

Think about when your sons are the most talkative. Are they chatty in the morning? Evening? Dinnertime? Bedtime? Whatever time it is, make it your best time too.

Squeezing Out Feelings

Getting boys to talk about their feelings is like squeezing lemon juice out of a lemon. First, the lemon has to be ripe and ready. Then, even with a lot of effort, you may get only a very little bit of juice. Expect boys to share a minuscule amount about how they feel, but be delighted when they do.

Michael Gurian, a well-known therapist and educator who has worked extensively with families and has written several books on boys such as *The Wonder of Boys*, wrote, "Because the two halves of the male brain are connected by a smaller group of fibers—the corpus callosum—than in the female brain, we can expect males in general to have greater difficulty than females expressing feelings."[2] Not that we shouldn't encourage boys to talk about feelings, but bear in mind that it's hardwired into boys' brains to have trouble describing feelings.

Gurian also suggests that parents can bother their boys by asking too often to describe their feelings. "Boys who are constantly asked how they feel will, for a while, feel good that their caregiver cares so much; but soon, if we just keep prodding the boy to talk about his feelings and he won't, what he's doing inside is building up resentment."[3]

Not long ago, Zane and I realized many of our family talks centered more on *what* we were doing rather than *how* we were doing. "Feeling" words had disappeared from our conversations. We asked a counselor for ideas on how to encourage our boys—and Zane and me—to talk about feelings.

She gave us a great idea, one that especially appealed to the boys.

She suggested conducting a friendly competition on who could use the most "feeling" words to describe his or her day in two minutes. For example, instead of saying, "I woke up this morning and went to school," we said, "I felt tired when I woke up, but when I took a shower I felt refreshed" and "At school I felt confused in math, but then once I understood the problem, I felt encouraged." We weren't allowed to use the same words repetitively, so we had a cheat sheet of feeling words to help guide us.

At first the boys thought it was ridiculous. And to be honest, it did feel a little awkward.

But Zane went first and started the ball rolling. We all wanted to beat him, because he always wins everything. The boys really got into it. They pulled out all sorts of feelings about their days—words we didn't even know existed in their vocabularies, such as *famished, ecstatic,* and *perplexed.* It was fun. After engaging in a conversation that went deeper than just "How was your day?" I felt as if I had tasted a sweet, cool, satisfying, glass of freshly squeezed lemonade—very content.

Exploring Their Worlds

All boys develop their own unique interests and personalities. Because each of our boys is different, how we communicate with each is different. The key is figuring out what makes each individual tick, his interests and his passions.

Once you figure that out, and it can change frequently, delve into that topic. For example, this year our youngest, Jake, learned about monarch butterflies in science class. His teacher brought in a chrysalis, and the class watched it transform into a butterfly and fly away. He became excited about this and wanted to do it at home. He asked his teacher where she found the chrysalis, and she told him that they're usually found on milkweed.

That evening, Jake and Zane made it a mission to find a monarch butterfly chrysalis on a milkweed and bring it home. For the next several days they searched fields, trails, and even spots along the road where milkweed flourished, but they didn't find any cocoons. Zane even called the Butterfly Pavilion, a tropical conservatory in Westminster, Colorado, filled with 1,200 free-flying butterflies imported from around the globe. They gave him useful information, such as the fact that the season for finding these cocoons was just ending. Although they never found the monarch butterfly chrysalis, the communication and bonding that took place between them was precious.

Finding a Girlfriend

A surefire technique of increasing boys' communication skills is something you can probably do nothing about as a parent. But when your son does develop a relationship with a girl, you might be pleasantly surprised. I have a friend whose son rarely spoke a word. She was worried about him. She even sought professional advice. Then he met a girl who became more than a friend. He spent hours on the phone with her. He took her on dates but not to movies, because he wanted to talk with her. He even baked her cupcakes that spelled out a special message.

He also became chattier at home. He opened up and shared more with his mom and dad. His mom saw his confidence increase and watched, amazed, as he matured into a young man who showed the type of communication skills she always hoped he would have. It's amazing what a girl can do.

Until your son reaches a point at which he chooses to communicate, keep reminding yourself that speaking few words shows wisdom. Eventually he'll evolve into a man who can articulate feelings, speak in grammatically correct sentences, look people in the eyes, and even express emotions. Meanwhile, be grateful to live in a home filled with very wise men of very few words.

Digging Deeper

I heard a joke about a boy who came upon the results of a study that said women use more words than men. Excited to prove to his mom that he had been right all along when he accused her of talking too much, he showed her the study results. It read, "Men use about 15,000 words per day, but women use 30,000."

The mom thought for a while and then finally she said to her son, "It's because we have to repeat everything we say."

"What?" the boy replied.

Ideas to Create Meaningful Conversations

Ask questions that require more than one-word answers. Instead of asking, "How was your day?" ask, "Who did you sit with at lunch today?"

Ask about your son's friends. Sometimes talking about friends will lead into a conversation about themselves.

Find an unusual story in the newspaper, and tell your son about it. Then ask him questions related to it.

Write down one thing your son is interested in. Commit to learning about it and conversing with him about it. (Hint: It's best to ask him questions and not try to show him what you know.)

Try the feelings competition with your own family. If you need help with "feeling" words, you can Google a list on the Internet.

Suggested Reading

Here are more thoughts from Proverbs about the value of using few words: Proverbs 10:19; Proverbs 17:27; Proverbs 21:23; Proverbs 29:20.

4. Technically Disadvantaged

"It was actually relatively simple," explains Ryan about a time when he was younger and played a joke on his babysitter. Using some advanced home technology, he created a situation that caused his babysitter to believe a burglar was breaking in.

"All I did was play a Halloween sound effects CD full of bumps, jumps, and ominous creaking sounds from the balcony, subtle enough that she couldn't tell where they were coming from," he said. "Next, I opened a window in the basement so it beeped and read on the security system."

"Was she scared?" I asked.

"Oh, yeah. She looked at me and said, 'Did you hear

that?' And I said, 'Hear what?' I made it faint enough that she wasn't sure she had heard anything. I stopped it before she ever figured it out."

"So your parents never even knew you did that?" I asked.

"No, but I did get caught the time I sent death threats to myself via my computer to our printer," Ryan mentioned

"*What?*" I asked.

"Well, there was this other time when I was being babysat, and I decided to scare this babysitter too. I was about 12 years old, and I think I was mad that my parents were still leaving me with babysitters. So I sent death threats to myself using our two computers and the printer."

"What did the threats say?"

"Something like 'Ryan, you'd better be careful when you come to school tomorrow. I've got a knife, and I'll be waiting for you.'"

"How did you make it believable?" I asked.

"Using the computer in the basement, I sent things to the upstairs printer. This was when almost no one knew a printer could be shared. I made them look like faxes, formatted with the correct numbers and readout at the top."

"How did she handle this?"

"She called my parents, who were out to dinner, and told them about the threats. She was about to call the police, but my parents decided to come home right away. Once my dad saw the threats, he figured out what I had done."

"I bet your parents weren't very happy," I commented.

"No, they grounded me from using my computer for at least two weeks—but I think that was the last time I ever had a babysitter." Ryan smiled.

Boys like Ryan are outsmarting their parents and/or babysitters with their superior knowledge of today's technology. Not all parents, though. Some of my friends are savvy with computers and other electronics and know much more than their kids know. However, I do have many friends who are somewhat clueless, like me. Technology is moving forward at a rapid pace, and it's a challenge to keep up.

Most of the time I feel technically disadvantaged in today's world. I've been told that I use about one-tenth of my computer's capacity—about the same amount, I've been told, that I use of my brain. I can't figure out how to work our new home sound system consisting of six different zones based on an iPod. I don't know how to record television programs. We occasionally stay at a friend's cabin in the mountains that has a home theater system. I'm terrified to touch the wrong button, because I'm afraid I'll mess it all up. But the boys know how to work it. I don't know how to use an electronic scheduler—I still use lots of sticky notes and a wall calendar.

I don't even know how to use my cell phone to its fullest capacity. Many times my boys have changed the settings on my phone, leaving me baffled about how to set it right again. One time Josh changed my ring-tone to his voice saying, "Mom, your phone is ringing; better answer it." Another time Jordan and a friend set my phone to show a photo of a man making a crazy face whenever Zane called. It took me a long time to figure out how to change my phone back to its original settings. But I'm slowly learning.

I'm committed to learning because I think it's essential to be knowledgeable about technology today. And I think we should encourage our sons to learn how to exist in this age and to be proficient in using computers and other electronics.

I'm embarrassed to confess that our family has been a bit slow in joining the electronic age. Just recently Zane purchased an iPod, and I have to admit, I love it. I keep wondering why we waited so long. Zane is a music buff, and he has put together great playlists. As I mentioned earlier, we use the iPod as our home sound system, but I also use it when I ride the stationary bike in our garage. It's so much fun. I feel as if I'm at a private concert with all my favorite songs.

Jordan, who's now 14, and Jake, 12, decided they wanted their own iPods. Using their savings, they each bought one. Their eyes have been opened to a whole new world. They get so excited about their new music that they want me to hear it. Some of the music is quite funky, such as the new techno music. At least I feel I'm familiar with what's popular among today's young people.

They also like to download ski videos. The other night Jake and I sat in front of the fire and, sharing his headphones, watched on his little screen a clip of the Armada ski team skiing at Whistler. Again, I loved it. We're experiencing something new together.

Zane and I also realized that we needed to set boundaries for the boys on using their iPods, because they seemed to be unwilling to detach from their newfound friend. Every time I looked at them, they had these little white wires dangling from their ears into various pockets. We decided we would not allow iPods at the dining table or during other social times and activities. The boys are also not allowed to purchase music on credit—they have to pay us at the time of purchase, and we must approve all music. So far these rules are working. Did I mention it's only been a week? I'm sure we'll have to make adjustments, but our attitude as parents is that it's fun. And it's part of their generation's culture.

Video games have especially captured boys' attention. As we all know, we live in a society that's much more technically advanced than the one in which most of us grew up. The sounds and graphics of video games are so enticing to boys that it's difficult to drag them away from the game. To make it even more entertaining, any boy with a high-speed Internet connection can play video games in real time against other gamers around the world.

In his book *Boys Adrift: The Five Factors Driving the Growing Epidemic of Unmotivated Boys and Underachieving Young Men*, Leonard Sax claims video games are one of the five culprits having a negative impact on boys today. He writes, "Sophisticated headsets allow boys to engage in simulated online combat in teams, arranging coordinated ambushes of enemy fighters using high-tech virtual weaponry. After your son has spent two hours leading a squad of fighters in a raid on terrorist headquarters, issuing commands through his headset-mounted microphone to his online comrades, and raced through a hail of virtual bullets to destroy the enemy power generator, well, studying Spanish grammar from a textbook can seem hopelessly dull."[1]

The point is that playing games is fun. Homework is boring compared to goofing around. But is this any different than when we were kids? Maybe the technology is more advanced and highly stimulating, but it's still the same concept.

So what do we do? Simple. Limit the time boys are allowed to play video games or engage in any electronic activity that distracts from family, friends, or homework. According to a 2005 survey done by the Kaiser Family Foundation, kids are spending 6.5 hours a day on the computer. Only 23 percent of the seventh- through twelfth-graders studied said their family has rules about computer activity. And just 17 percent say they have restrictions on video game time. As responsible parents, we should attempt to increase that percentage. It's okay, even admirable, to set limits.

What's a reasonable amount of time? That's up to each family to decide, based on each boy's personality, grades, and other factors. If our boys are not doing well in school, they're not allowed to play video or computer games during the weeknights and only for a limited time on the weekends. We've found that to be a useful carrot to dangle in front of them. If they're doing well in school, we limit watching television or playing video and/or computer games to one hour a night and are more lenient on the weekends.

As a technically disadvantaged adult, I have to make a tremendous effort to be knowledgeable about the current technology involving video games, iPods, text messaging, and other electronics that capture my boys' attention. Because I don't want to be clueless, I try to be informed. I've learned how to use the iPod, although I'm still working on using it with our sound system. I'm learning more about my computer. I know how to text message, and I'm learning more about my cell phone. Did you know many cell phones have a built-in tip calculator? It's awesome. I occasionally—well, rarely—play Xbox games with the boys, even though they make me motion sick and I always lose. However, I do get a kick out of watching them and their friends play. They make the most bizarre faces when they're concentrating on shooting aliens.

I think when boys are totally engaged in video or computer games, they become zombie-like. *Zombie* is defined in Dictionary.com as "the body of a dead person given the semblance of life but mute and will-less, by a supernatural force." Sound familiar? When playing electronic games, boys disengage from real life and become absorbed in the make-believe world of the game. It's weird! I feel as if I'm talking to a mute, will-less person whose body has been overtaken by a supernatural force—the game. It's almost impossible to talk to a boy while he's playing a video or computer game. To get one of my boys' attention, I have to touch his shoulder and ask him to look at me. When I'm done speaking, I ask him to repeat to me what I just said.

Elinor Ochs, director of UCLA's Center on Everyday Lives of Families, has studied how the electronic culture is changing family life. She notes, "We saw how difficult it was for parents to penetrate the child's universe. We have so many videotapes of parents actually backing away, retreating from kids who are absorbed by whatever they're doing."[2]

As an example of this phenomenon, my friend Amy shared a story about her seven-year-old son, Luke, and how he became so engrossed in a game that he didn't notice the house was on fire.

Luke was downstairs playing on his PlayStation when his little brother, Carter, came inside and turned on the gas fireplace right next to Luke. Carter was cold and wanted to warm up his shirt. He hung his shirt up next to the fire and went into another room to fool around. The shirt was too close to the fireplace, and it caught on fire. Luke was oblivious. He didn't notice the flames, feel the heat, or smell the smoke—he just kept right on playing.

Amy, who was upstairs in the kitchen, smelled the smoke. Their fire alarms were disabled, because the batteries were dead and she hadn't replaced them yet. She ran downstairs and saw the fire. She hollered at Luke and Carter to get outside. Luke looked at her as if she were crazy. She forced him out the back door, then turned on the garden hose, filled up a bucket with water, ran back inside, and extinguished the fire. Unbelievable? Not really. If you have boys who get lost in playing video games, you understand.

The mesmerizing effect video games have on boys is not only when boys are young. I know adult men who play them all night. One friend has had to limit her husband's game time to one night a week. Also, some teenage boys prefer to play video games rather than be with a girlfriend— and girls aren't putting up with it. In a *New York Times* article titled "At Colleges, Women Are leaving Men in the Dust," a young woman describes how her boyfriend played video games at least four hours a day. He told her he would try to cut back to 15 hours a week, but that wasn't good enough for her. That's the same amount of time she spent at a paid internship. She ended the relationship. "That's my litmus test now," she said. "I won't date anyone who plays video games. It means they're choosing to do something that wastes their time and sucks the life out of them." [3]

Although they can be addicting for boys, I don't think video games are all bad. If used in moderation, they can be fun. With a little creativity, they can even engage the entire family. In his book *Boys Adrift*, Dr. Sax shares a positive experience of playing video games with his kids. He writes, "I own a GameBike. It looks like an ordinary exercise bike, but it plugs into a PlayStation and functions just like a game controller—except that if you want your virtual motorcycle to go faster, you don't press a button, you pedal faster. Kids around the neighborhood love to come over and play against Dr. Sax on video games like "MTX Motocross" and "NASCAR: Dirt to Daytona." They always win; they can push the buttons faster than I can pedal." [4]

To some, technology is scary or evil, but it doesn't have to be. Jesus mentions several times in the Book of John, chapter 17, that we as Christians live "in the world," but he cautions Christians not to be "of the world." To me, this means we don't have to fear technology. We live in the world and need to know how to function. We can embrace the advances in technology and stay informed about the newest games, gadgets, and Internet opportunities as long as we don't let them be all-consuming.

Below are some guidelines to help you keep up with what your boys are into and help protect them from the potential dangers of today's electronic culture.

Know what games your boys are playing. Caution: A few video games—"Grand Theft Auto" and "Doom" to name a couple, contain antisocial, aggressive content. These games encourage killing police, women, and innocent bystanders. These types of games should not be in our homes.

Know what music your boys like. Pay attention to the words more than the sounds. Some current music might sound horrible to you, but if the words are good, it's probably okay.

Know what movies they're watching.

Know whom they're Instant Messaging (IMing) and what they're saying. Let your kids know you'll occasionally be reading their messages.

Know if they have My Space or Face Book, and if they do, check it out. If you don't like what you see, remember: you're the parent. Get rid of it.

Know how to text message with your cell phone. Most kids prefer to communicate with their parents using text messaging—they never listen to voice messages anyway. Texting also takes away the awkwardness of talking to Mom or Dad on the phone in front of friends.

Install a computer program such as "Safe Eyes" to block inappropriate and unwanted images. Programs such as this protect your boys from Web sites you don't want them to visit. Pornography is a huge temptation, and it's easily accessible to anyone anytime. Protect your boys by making it difficult to access objectionable Web sites.

Keep the computer in a public place in your home. Your son will be less likely to visit inappropriate Web sites with you in the room.

Encourage your boys to be proficient at using the advanced technology our world offers. Have fun with it. Just be cautious, and don't let the technology control them—or you.

Digging Deeper

A dad of three boys said, "My boys don't do anything like what I did when I was a kid. Making forts was big. My kids have never made a fort. You know, grab a bunch of pillows and blankets, go in the basement, and build a cool fort."

Can you relate?

Have an electronic-free night—or week or month. Spend time with your boys building a fort with blankets and pillows.

Get Real About Technology

On a scale of 1 to 10—1 being "not very" and 10 being "very" knowledgeable—how knowledgeable are you about using current technology?

Investigate to see what specific steps you can take to learn more.

Get educated about technology, and set fair limits for your boys regarding the use of electronics.

What does it mean to you to be "in the world" but "not of the world" in regard to today's technology?

Suggested Reading

Other scriptures to consider: Proverbs 27:23; Matthew 10:16; John 17:15-26.

5. Urban Safari

The Pursuit of Adventure

During the fourth watch of the night Jesus went out to them,
walking on the lake. When the disciples saw him walking on the lake,
they were terrified. "It's a ghost," they said, and cried out in fear.
But Jesus immediately said to them: "Take courage! It is I.
Don't be afraid." "Lord, if it's you," Peter replied, "tell me
to come to you on the water." "Come," he said.
—Matthew 14:25-29

"Dad!" Jordan's voice sounded terrified through the phone. "Can you come over here? We think there's a bear in the alley."

It isn't unusual to spot a bear in our neighborhood. We live near the foothills, and bears tend to venture into our area in search of food, especially in the fall when they're trying to eat hundreds of pounds of grub each day to prepare for their long winter naps. But it's still a bit scary.

"What's going on?" Zane asked.

"Can you just come over here, please? We were playing outside and heard some growling and banging around the trashcans in the alley. We think a bear is out there."

"Where are you now?" Zane asked. It was 9:30 P.M. and very dark outside.

"We're all inside," he reassured Zane.

Zane found our two boys and six neighborhood kids huddled in our neighbors' home. The parents had gone out for a late dinner and hadn't answered their cell phones.

When I married Zane, I knew he was a guy who loves a good thrill. In fact, I would classify him as a type "T" personality—a "thrill seeker." When he heard a bear might be nearby, he wanted to see it.

He piled all eight kids into our minivan and drove around to the alley. It was dark outside, but they had flashlights shining through the van windows as they searched for signs of a bear.

They didn't see one in the alley behind the house, but Zane is not one to give up easily. He decided to keep looking. He began driving up and down the alleys in our neighborhood. It became an urban safari. The kids anticipated seeing a bear around each corner or trashcan. They saw skunks and raccoons, but no bears.

Then Zane expanded the search area. He drove down a cul-de-sac a few blocks from our house. Near the end of the street he and Jordan spotted something very large and tan. It jumped a fence and disappeared into one of our neighbor's yards.

"That was a mountain lion," Zane whispered.

"I saw it too," Jordan confirmed.

"It was probably just a fox," one of the boys commented.

"No way," Zane said. "It was too big for a fox." A mountain lion had recently been sighted in our neck of the woods, but they're very elusive.

Zane pulled up in front of the home. He wanted to warn the neighbors of the dangerous animal prowling in their backyard. As he got out of the car to ring the doorbell, the kids called out to him to be careful. The family answered the door and said they were grateful for the warning because they had two small children and a dog.

"Let's go find that lion," Zane said to the kids when he got back into the car.

I asked him to describe the adventure in his own words:

The excitement in the car was like an electric current running through all of our bodies. I could feel the kids' anticipation. The windows were open, but they didn't want to scare the lion off, so the kids were silent as we searched. I drove up near a trailhead just a block from our home and stopped in front of the spot where the trail meets the sidewalk. The home situated at the end of our street, next to the trail, has a motion light mounted above the garage door. Suddenly, the light came on as a HUGE mountain lion jumped the black iron gate and sauntered up the long driveway toward the garage. We all held our breath. It was unbelievable. The lion stopped, turned its head, and glared at us. Then he slowly strutted away into the darkness beyond the home and into the forest.

The moment he was out of sight, the kids in the car just started screaming. We were high-fiving each other, celebrating the amazing sight of a real live, wild, mountain lion roaming our neighborhood. I think this will be a memory the kids and I will have forever.

I so wish I had been with them! Jake said he could see the muscles rippling on the mountain lion's sides and the black tip of his tail. He told me that seeing the mountain lion was so exciting that it changed his life.

That's the power of adventure. Experiencing adventure with your boys can be life-changing.

What is adventure?

Adventure for some means risky or dangerous behavior. Experiencing adventure can become addictive. Some people seek the adrenaline rush, but the rush lasts only a moment. Then the need for another rush leads them to do a more dangerous stunt, sometimes putting their lives or the lives of others in jeopardy.

Because I love to write true adventure stories, I've been privileged to interview many people who have taken adventure to the extreme and were fortunate to be alive and to be telling me their stories. In many cases, those people had made poor decisions in order to satisfy their need for adrenalin. For example, I interviewed guys who survived an avalanche and still regret their decision to ski out of bounds. I also interviewed mountain climbers who witnessed their companions swept off Mt. Everest by a mighty wind in their quest to conquer that peak. They lament the fact that they did not heed the warning of a severe storm headed in their direction.

I was also fortunate to interview Aron Ralston, who was trapped under a boulder in a canyon in Utah and made the decision to amputate his own arm to escape. He admits that he made some terrible mistakes. In his book *Between a Rock and a Hard Place*, he describes how he felt about some of his decisions. At one point he videotaped himself, telling his parents and sister he loved them. He writes, "I go out looking for adventure and risk so I can feel alive. But I go out by myself, and I don't tell anyone where I'm going. That's just dumb. If someone knew, if I'd have been with someone else, there would probably already be help on the way. Even if I'd just talked to a ranger or left a note on my truck. Dumb, dumb, dumb."[1]

I am not encouraging families to pursue the type of adventure that puts your boys' lives at risk and encourages them to lead a life of recklessness. It's not my goal to raise adrenaline junkies. But I am suggesting making healthy adventure a way of life for your family, instilling in your boys the truth that *life* is an adventure. I believe boys need to experience adventure to thrive.

Adventure is defined by Dictionary.com as "an exciting or very unusual experience." I like this definition, because it's simple and makes adventure possible any time and any place. You don't have to sign up for an expensive family vacation hiking, biking, whitewater rafting, elephant trekking, or living in a tree house in Thailand to create escapades with your boys.

You can create an adventure on any day anywhere, such as the kitchen. We encourage the boys to be adventurous in cooking. They create smoothies, sauces for ice cream, and their own special pies filled with chocolate chips, coconut, walnuts, and sweetened condensed milk. They actually won a pie contest with their creation one Fourth of July.

The boys have transformed our house into a dark, scary

place for a game called "Sardines," in which one person hides and the others have to find him in the dark without saying a word. When they find the person's hiding place, they hide with him until one person is wandering alone in the dark house, scared out of his wits, looking for everyone else.

Your neighborhood can be a great place of discovery. Our boys also play a game called "Bigger and Better." They start with a paper clip and visit neighbors, asking to trade the paper clip for something bigger and better. Because we have some college rentals in our neighborhood, the boys have come home with some interesting treasures that include Tiki torches, a gigantic never-used kite, a three-foot strobe light, and even a large television set.

Most boys are infatuated with insects. Bugs and boys are a sure recipe for simple, everyday adventures. Jake was not only infatuated with bugs when he was younger, but he also had an unusual interest in eating them. One day he found a caterpillar and decided to put it in on the grill as we cooked hamburgers. He proceeded to dip it in ketchup and eat it. He said it didn't taste bad. In fact, he said, it tasted a little like lemonade. For him, this was an adventure—an unusual, exciting experience. For me it was absolutely disgusting, and for Zane and the other boys it was pure entertainment.

I wouldn't be surprised if someday one or all of my boys are on some new version of the popular TV show "Man Versus Wild," which, by the way, I think is so popular because kids today watch other people's adventures since they aren't engaged in any adventures of their own. Many boys spend time playing computer and Xbox games to feed their need for excitement, a kind of warped way of getting it without experiencing it in real life. They view adventure through a box rather than through the old-fashioned, get-out-of-your-house-and-do-something type of activity.

Live in the Moment

When Zane and I were engaged, Father Don, the priest from my childhood Episcopal church, required us to meet with him a few times for premarital counseling. This was one of the best things we ever did to build a strong foundation for our marriage. At the time, Father Don was dying from cancer, and he knew it. We cling to one piece of advice he gave us: "Don't live life anticipating the exciting moments, the holidays, and the vacations, but enjoy each day you're given." Make the ordinary day extraordinary—every day. We're not always successful at this concept, and sometimes we waste a day being angry at each other, but living this way is our goal, and we hope to pass it on to our boys.

Luci Swindoll writes in her book *I Married Adventure,*

The most interesting people I know drink in life and savor every drop—the sweet and the sour. The good and the bad. The planned and the unplanned. And isn't that what God intends? When Jesus modeled humanity for you and me to see, he was out there—everywhere! He took risks. He embraced life and responded to everyone and everything, the tender and the tumultuous. His capacity for life was without measure. And we are designed like him—fully human and fully alive.

She concludes this thought by writing, "Capturing the moment is a choice, a way of life. It requires us to wake up, live life, and be present—here, there, and everywhere."[2]

What an awesome gift to give your boys: the gift of living each day with a sense of adventure, living each moment to its fullest potential. As the psalmist wrote, "This is the day the LORD has made; let us rejoice and be glad in it" (Psalm 118:24).

Step Out of Your Comfort Zone

The disciple Peter was a person with an adventurous spirit. I can only wonder what he was like as a little boy. He probably got himself into all sorts of trouble with his "do-it-before-thinking" personality. I love the story of Peter's walking on water. When Jesus said, "Come," Peter didn't hesitate. He stepped out of the boat and onto the lake. He experienced a miracle—he walked on water! If he hadn't risked stepping out of the boat, out of his comfort zone, he wouldn't have personally experienced something supernatural.

Can you imagine walking on water in the dark, in a windstorm, toward Jesus? The closest I've felt to walking on water is water skiing, which for me is an incredible experience until I fall and hit the water so hard it makes my eyelashes flip inside my eyelids. It's not pretty, but I still get up and go again. When Peter panicked, he sank. But Jesus immediately grabbed his hand, pulled him up and into the boat, and even calmed the wind.

I imagine Peter felt a little humiliated, but my guess is he felt more exhilarated because he walked on water, even just a few steps. Later in life, this experience must have increased his faith and helped him trust God to do miracles through him such as healing blind, sick, and paralyzed people, and catching a fish with a coin in its mouth to pay his taxes! Peter's life was definitely an adventure.

For each person, stepping out of his or her comfort zone is different. For some it's taking a walk in the dark with a flashlight; for others it might be wearing pajamas and going out for ice cream. For others it might be backpacking 10 miles to a lake to camp and fish or riding 100 miles on a mountain bike. It doesn't matter what level of adventure fits you and your family, but it does matter that you make it a significant, memorable part of your family life.

Girls Allowed

Experiencing adventure should not be exclusive to boys. Moms and daughters, don't be left behind! I wish I had been with the boys when they spotted the mountain lion. But to be honest, I was in bed reading a good book when Jordan called. Zane asked me if I wanted to go, and I said no because I didn't want to leave the warmth of my comfy bed. At other times I've gone on—-even initiated—an adventure, and I've never regretted it.

I see many families who encourage dads and boys to be adventurous, which is great, but it makes me sad when the gals aren't encouraged to participate too. It takes a conscious effort to step out of our comfort zones, but the results are the same for females as they are for males. Adventure makes life interesting and exciting and creates meaningful, sometimes very humorous, family memories and stories for a lifetime.

I have a friend who was visiting a crocodile preserve in Florida with her five-year-old son and husband. They were listening to a man talk about the crocodiles. A 12-foot crocodile with a four-foot snout lounged on the sand nearby. As the man spoke, the beast opened his jaws and showed his sharp teeth. It was easy to imagine how, with one bite he could swallow a child. His neck had a rope around it, tied to a pole, so he couldn't move much.

"Who wants to come and sit on this croc?" the man asked.

"Yeah, right. Who in their right might is going to be dumb enough to do that?" my friend whispered to her husband.

At the same time her little boy's hand shot into the air. "I do!" he screamed.

The man pointed to her son. Shocked, she watched her blond little boy waltz up to the prehistoric looking monster. Her husband, not wanting to miss out on the action, jogged right out there too. Together they sat down on its scaly back. She has a picture of them with big grins on their faces sitting on the back of a crocodile in the sand.

"Next time, I'm going to go, too—I don't want to be left out of the picture," she commented. Remember, girls—if you can't beat 'em, join 'em.

Be imaginative in creating adventure for your sons. Hike to the tops of mountains. Go camping, especially in the rain. Look for snakes under rocks. Sneak through the neighborhood playing "Capture the Flag." Sleep under the stars. Eat waffles topped with strawberries and whipped cream for dinner. Jump into an ice-cold lake. Go bowling at midnight. Bike out to breakfast. Do flips off the high-dive. Buy chocolate-covered grasshoppers, and dare everyone in the family to eat one.

Even if it's against your nature, try not to squelch your

boys' appetite for adventure. Let them feel alive and experience what life has to offer. Why not?

Digging Deeper

Life is a daring adventure or nothing.
—Helen Keller.

Something to Think About

Do you consider your life a daring adventure? If not, what can you do differently on a daily basis to make life more of an adventure?

Plan an adventure for your family, and do it.

Here are some adventure stories in the Bible:

Samson's story: Judges 14—16

David's story: 1 Samuel 16-30

Daniel's story: The Book of Daniel

Paul's story: Acts 27—28

Suggested Reading

The Dangerous Book for Boys, by Conn Iggulden and Hal Iggulden.

Endurance: Shackleton's Incredible Voyage, by Alfred Lansing.

6. Boys and Sports

*Since we are surrounded by such a great cloud of witnesses,
let us throw off everything that hinders and the sin that so
easily entangles, and let us run with perseverance the race
marked out for us. Let us fix our eyes on Jesus.*
—Hebrews 12:1-2

"Mom, I'm giving up soccer for paintball," 13-year-old Josh announced as he waltzed in from his first paintball outing. He had a wide grin on his face, and he was covered from head to foot in camouflage clothing speckled with green, yellow, and orange paint splotches. He wiped his sweaty forehead with his dirt-covered hands.

"What?" I asked.

"Paintball is sooo fun, and it's good exercise. I want to play competitive paintball." He reached into the fridge, grabbed a purple Gatorade, and downed it.

"Josh, paintball is not a sport," I responded. *Is he kidding?* I wondered.

"Yes, it is. There are competitions all over the United States."

"Yeah, right—probably a bunch of guys who like to shoot at little kids," I said half-jokingly.

"Mom, I'm serious."

"Well, I still don't think you can call paintball a sport. If it were considered an official sport, it would be in the Olympics, right?"

"Mom, come on," he said and rolled his eyes at me. "Kids are getting into it all over the place. You can win really cool stuff like paintball guns, masks, CO_2 tanks, even cash prizes sometimes."

"I don't think any colleges give away paintball scholarships," I mentioned. "And it's probably really expensive."

"I would use my allowance to help pay for it. And think of the money you'd save if you weren't paying for soccer."

"Good point," I admitted. Last year, and during several previous years, we had spent more than $2,000 on his soccer. It would be nice to save a little money. But the real question I had to ask was "Why don't you want to play soccer?"

"It's just not fun anymore," he replied, shrugging his shoulders.

I had heard that at about age 13 boys start dropping out of competitive sports. According to the Institute of Youth Sports at Michigan State, close to 70 percent of all kids who play organized sports stop playing sports entirely by the time they turn 13. But I hadn't imagined my kids would be a part of that statistic.

"Why isn't it fun anymore?" I asked.

"I don't know—I just want to try something new," Josh answered. He had been playing soccer since he was four years old, which meant he had been playing it for nine years! Many grown-ups I know don't keep the same job that long. *No wonder he's ready for a change*, I thought.

After talking to him a bit more about why he wasn't having fun, I discovered he also felt too much pressure. Regardless of whether the pressure was self-imposed or was coming from us or his coaches, it was a huge factor in fun depletion.

Soccer demanded most of his free time, and he wanted to do some other things—like paintball. Going out with his buddies and blasting each other with multicolored paint was simply fun. He felt no pressure to perform and had no adults telling him what to do, how to play, or how to get better and win more. And I couldn't argue about the exercise. He was definitely sweaty and smelly!

We decided, in Josh's case, that one sport had become too serious too soon. He was burned out at 13. After many discussions, we realized Josh needed a break from the intensity of competitive soccer, and, frankly, so did we.

The days of hanging out with our neighbors on the sidelines, drinking coffee, eating bagels, socializing, and half-way watching our preschool-aged boys and girls play soccer seemed like a lifetime ago. Now we generally sat hunched in our fold-out chairs or paced the sidelines with the other uptight, nail-biting parents.

So we sat down with Josh and came up with a plan. He wanted to play soccer, but just for fun. We talked to his coach and requested that he be placed on a less competitive, more recreational team. Instead of practicing three times a week with a fourth "optional" practice and games on the weekends *and* committing to winter indoor soccer *and* the spring league *and* at least one out-of-state tournament, he had time to pursue other interests. He played football at the park with his friends, he skied as much as possible—80 times that year—learned to scuba dive, played tennis, and swam in our neighbor's backyard pool with our new puppy.

I know we're not the only people discouraged with youth sports in America. I've talked to many parents of boys who wish things were different. Most parents have had to console a heartbroken son who didn't get placed on the team he had hoped to make during tryouts. And I'm not talking about high school boys—I'm talking about 10-year-olds. Most elite travel teams start holding tryouts for children that age. Kids are giving up on themselves with sports way too early because they don't make the competitive teams. Moving up to a team is hard once they've been placed lower on the totem pole, and they feel humiliated. Many boys would just rather not play.

I've interviewed many parents of boys who faced the same dilemma we did. Their boys wanted to try a different sport or didn't want to commit to a single sport year-round but were being forced to commit or quit. Children shouldn't have to make that kind of decision at such an early age—or at any age, really.

If you feel like Zane and me and many other parents of boys who want their boys to develop a lifelong love of sports and keep "play" the emphasis, here are some suggestions for you to employ in your family.

Life-changing Tips for Parents with Boys in Sports

Keep sports fun. Frequently ask your son if he's having fun.

Don't specialize in a single sport before high school. I would prefer to say *never* select a single sport, but if your child desires to specialize in a sport, then high school is the time to select one and go for it.

Interview coaches about their philosophies such as play time, discipline, goals, financial expectations, and other things that are important to you.

Care about other kids, not just your own. Sports should be fun for all children, not just the naturally gifted. Also, make an effort to cheer for the entire team, not just your own child.

Regard sports as a tool for fitness and an opportunity for character growth. Keep in mind your goal for your child in sports. Is it to develop character qualities such as teamwork, persistence, commitment, and fitness, or is it to become number one, play college or professional sports, and earn fame and fortune?

Focus on relationships. If you can't have a normal conversation with your spouse or other parents on the sidelines during your child's sporting activity because you're so focused on the game, then you're taking it too seriously. The parents of the boys your son plays with are put into your path for a reason. They may never sit by you in church, but they'll sit with you on the sidelines of a game and chat. They'll observe your attitudes and behavior. You can have a positive or a negative effect on their lives based on how you relate during this time with others. Don't forget your spouse. It should be fun to watch your boys play sports. It can be marriage-building, memory-making, and all sorts of good stuff. Make sure it's not a negative experience.

Speak encouraging words. Don't embarrass or humiliate your son with comments during games and after the game. One coach I spoke to suggested parents don't even talk about the game for 24 hours unless their son brings it up. He also suggested not focusing the conversation on performance but emphasizing effort. Remember—you have the power to build your son up with words or tear him down.

Control what you say about other players, coaches, and referees. I interviewed a soccer referee who told me some of the unbelievable comments adults make to him: "You're an idiot!" "How many of the players do you know on the other team?" "What a homer you are!" "You're not keeping up with the play because you're too slow." And that's not the worst of them.

On the other hand, he did give me some positive examples of comments adults made to him: "You did a great job keeping this game in control. Well done." "You know, you've done several of our games the last few seasons. And every time you show up, I know we're going to get a fair shake at the game." He added, "When I have parents, players, and coaches from the losing team say 'good game' and 'thanks,' I know it's been a good day."

Balance is the key. Is one sport dominating your family life? Do you find you *never* get to have a family dinner because of sports? If the answer is yes, it might be time to rethink the commitment to this sport and to reestablish priorities.

Keep playing your own sport. It's true that parents live vicariously through their children, especially in athletics. It's very difficult not to let your child's successes or failures become a reflection of you, so it's important for parents to keep sports in their own lives. This will not only help you deemphasize your son's experiences but will also set a good example to your boys of a lifetime of fitness.

Don't go to every game. I think it's healthful to miss a game once in a while, because this takes some pressure off your son if he's feeling pressured from you in sports.

Keep sports fun! This is so important that I had to emphasize it twice—which probably isn't enough.

Bob Bigelow, the author of *Just Let the Kids Play: How to Stop Other Adults from Ruining Your Child's Fun and Success in Youth Sports*, writes jokingly that adults would turn any childhood activity, even tag, into a competition if they could. Read what Bigelow had to say:

> The adults would start with their basic needs for organization and management. They would find the fields, organize teams, set schedules. If the kids were going to play tag, obviously they'd need adults to tell them how to play. They'd need coaches. The coaches would need assistant coaches to keep track of tag minutes, tag assists, and tag hits. The coaches would need to figure out how to beat the other tag teams.[1]

You know, it's not that crazy of a notion. I recently heard about cup-stacking as a competitive sport. I don't know all the rules, but basically a player is timed as he or she stacks and unstacks cups in a specific sequence or pattern. It's officially called "sport stacking," and the Web site <www.worldsportstackingassociation.org> shows amazing videos of a 10-year-old boy from the United States who set the new world record, 7.23 seconds, on October 20, 2007. This kid is lightning fast—his hands move so quickly they're a blur.

If you want to know more, the rules, tournaments, and other information of the sport are outlined on the Web site, which even promotes products such as special cups. For a meager $30 you can purchase performance-enhancing cups, even cups that glow in the dark to increase your child's chances at the next world cup event. Honestly, this looks like a lot of fun. I think my boys have had a P.E. unit on cup stacking, and it does develop great hand-eye coordination, but is it really necessary to crown a cup-stacking world champion?

We can't change America's obsession with specialization in youth sports, but we can shape our own family's philosophy about sports. Put into practice the words found in Hebrews 12:1-2—"Since we are surrounded by such a great cloud of witnesses, let us throw off everything that hinders and the sin that so easily entangles, and let us run with perseverance the race marked out for us. Let us fix our eyes on Jesus." We can set an example in our own communities as families who participate in sports but don't let sports rule our lives.

We can fight to keep an eternal perspective and not get caught up in the sports moment. We can choose to impact those we come in contact with in youth sports for the positive and to use sports as a tool to develop character in our kids. We can show those around us that sports are fun. Even though our culture has created a somewhat dysfunctional system with youth sports, let's do our individual best to put the fun back in dysFUNctional.

Digging Deeper

A survey of parents at the National PTA convention in 2004 found that 92 percent of parents polled said that sports were either important or very important to their children's overall development. Of those same parents polled, 44 percent revealed that their children had quit playing a sport because it was no longer making them happy.

Also, 56 percent of those parents said that youth sports had become too competitive, that the coaches had been too focused on winning, and that organized youth sports need to be totally revamped in terms of priorities.

Questions for Reflection

Do you agree or disagree with the parents mentioned above? Why or why not?

What is your parental philosophy about your boys and sports?

Write down what you hope your son will learn through participating in sports. Keep these goals in mind as your son grows and has successes and failures in his athletic career.

Ask your son if he's happy and having fun. If the answer is no, ask him what you can do to help him keep sports fun in his life. Remember to ask him these questions frequently.

Suggested Reading

Just Let the Kids Play, by Bob Bigelow, Tom Moroney, and Linda Hall.

Here are some scriptures to encourage parents of athletes: Ephesians 4:29; Philippians 3:12-14; Colossians 3:1-4.

7. Think Pink
The Art of Being a Girl While You're Raising Boys

As iron sharpens iron, so one man [or woman] sharpens another.
—Proverbs 27:17

I am not a girly-girl.

I enjoy watching sports. I like mountain biking. I don't care much for shopping. I enjoy eating a good steak and reading the sports page. And I love being a mom of boys. I believe God knew what he was doing when he blessed me with three of them. But I'm still a girl, and girls have specific needs that are unique to the feminine gender.

There are facets of my personality that only another female can truly understand. For example, the boys don't understand why I like to put on Burt's Bees Green Clay Mask and lie on my bed with cucumber slices on my eyes, color my hair a variety of different shades of brown, watch a romantic movie, soak in a bubble bath, wear high-heels, take an hour to get ready to go out, hide personal stashes of chocolate around the house, and get grumpy once a month.

As hard as Zane and the boys try to be sensitive to me, at times I throw up my hands in exasperation. They still drink from the milk carton, eat with their hands instead of forks, laugh about bodily emissions, and, of course, there's the whole toilet lid issue.

They are boys. I am a girl.

When I feel overwhelmed by boys, I simply need to be with girls. This is one reason God gave us each other. Don't misunderstand me—I believe our husbands and children will meet many, even most, of our needs. But it's okay to find fulfillment and understanding in being around other girls. It's more than okay—it's highly recommended.

A nurses' health study from Harvard Medical School found that the more friends women have, the less likely they are to develop physical impairments as they age, and the more likely they are to be leading joyful lives. The results were so significant that the researchers concluded that not having close friends or confidants was as detrimental to your health as smoking or carrying extra weight.[1].

Girl Talk

One important need all women have is to talk with other women. I have a friend with three boys who keeps a little Barbie doll on her kitchen windowsill. Her Barbie sports a bikini top and a grassy hula skirt. My friend named her Wilson, in honor of the volleyball that became Tom Hanks' silent companion for the 1,500 days he was stranded on a deserted island in the movie *Castaway*. My friend talks to

Wilson when she is needs a little female interaction. Although her Wilson is not a living, breathing female friend, she still feels comforted when she talks to her.

How much better, then, to have real-live girlfriends to talk with when we yearn for female companionship! In Laura Jensen Walker's book *Girl Time: A Celebration of Chick Flicks, Bad Hair Days, and Good Friends*, she writes, "We women have a connection, an inexplicable bond that men simply can't share. And talking is a huge part of that."[2] I have several outlets to help meet my need for girl talk.

One, I'm in a Bible study once a week with close friends who have become an incredible source of strength and encouragement. We have lived through unbelievable ups and downs. At times we've laughed until our sides hurt.

And at other times we've held each other up when we couldn't stand up on our own because life had knocked us down so hard. We frequently mention to each other that we don't know how we would get through life without this supportive group.

I also have several friends I bike, hike, or run with. This time of exercising and talking together truly feeds my soul. A woman once told me, "Be careful whom you work out with, because you end up sharing at a deeper level than you do at other times." I've noticed she's right. Something about a long ride or a long run causes conversations to reach a deeper and more meaningful level. Connecting with other women in such a profound manner fills a hole in my spirit.

Another woman I meet with is Judy; she has walked through life a little ahead of me. We have a special friendship, and there is a unique bond between us. She meets my need to connect with another woman in a mentoring type of relationship. We often take our dogs on walks together, and I ask her advice, and we share prayer requests. Sometimes she makes me a bowl of oatmeal with yogurt, nuts, and fresh peaches, and we sit on her back porch and chat. One time we took a five-hour bike ride together and talked the entire five miles. As a mentor, prayer partner, and friend, she's a treasure to me. We've been meeting together for almost nine years now, and I look forward to many more years together.

Girl Time

Girl talk and girl time go hand in hand. But I'm suggesting that you make an intentional effort to plan girlfriend getaways—a significant dose of girl time. A few years back, I went with a group of girlfriends to Santa Barbara to take surfing lessons. We hired an instructor who tried to teach us how to surf—bless his heart. Each morning we would drag the surfboards off the top of the car, over the railroad tracks, and onto Santa Claus Beach, where we would set up for the day. Our instructor spent a couple of hours a day with us, then left us to practice on our own.

I tried and tried to ride a wave. I had sore arms and stomach muscles from propping myself up on the board. I had bruises and scrapes on my sides from lying on the board while I waited for the perfect wave. We later learned that we were taking our lessons during the worst season for good waves. I practically got hypothermic from the time immersed in the cold water. Because I was so chilled, I decided to wear two wetsuits while surfing. I looked like a chubby seal, but I didn't care, because I knew my friends loved me no matter how ridiculous I looked.

I never did get the hang of surfing, but the time we shared floating out in the ocean on our surfboards while dolphins swam by, incessantly talking and laughing, then finishing the day with a fire on the beach and eating shortbread dipped in Nutella, gave me a much-needed time with just the girls. This focused time of playing together joined our spirits in a deep way, created lifelong memories, and energized me to come home and be the wife and mom I'm meant to be.

Another girls' getaway I cherish was when my mom took my two sisters and me on vacation to Mexico for an entire week. At the time, my sisters and I all had little kids we left behind at home. It was hard to arrange all the details to make this vacation work, but it was absolutely worth the effort. It took me about five seconds to relax once we arrived at our hotel. We lounged on the beach, snorkeled, and even went to a hilarious late-night show. We laughed so hard we had to leave.

Sometimes it's too difficult or expensive to get away for a whole vacation, but even a sleepover together or an afternoon of shopping or an hour at a coffee shop is rejuvenating and inspiring. For me, it's a needed boost when I'm feeling I need a little more pink in my life.

A Room of Your Own

Having a space for you is not a new idea. In *A Room of One's Own*, written in 1929, Virginia Woolf suggests every woman needs a room of her own in order to have the freedom to create. I agree with Woolf: creating a space for yourself gives you a place to be you. One of my good friends, Mary Ellen, who co-owns the popular women's clothing line, Fresh Produce Sportswear, with her husband, Thom, has two boys the same ages as my two youngest. We often laugh together about our similar lives: we both love cinnamon bears, we married only a week apart the same year, we had our boys only a week apart the same years, and we even chose the same names. We often share parallel experiences of raising boys, such as watching them win and lose on the same teams, attend the same schools, struggle through the same homework assignments, complain about the same girls, and get into the same trouble throwing snowballs at the mailman. We also share our similar need to nurture our feminine spirits in the midst of mothering boys.

Mary Ellen, along with Virginia Woolf, inspired me with the idea of creating a room of my own. One Sunday evening, after a weekend of watching the boys play a zillion basketball games, Mary Ellen decided she needed a place in her own home just for her, a place to retreat after an infusion of boy activities. She selected an upstairs room with an incredible view of the mountains and delegated moving to the basement the workout equipment that filled the room. Then she painted the room a bright, cheerful pink. She set up her sewing machine and uses this space to relax and rejuvenate her feminine spirit. She even uses this room to create the new line of women's clothes that she feels reflects her heart.

I don't have a pink room, but I do have a small loft where I read, write, and pray. This space gives me a place to create, grow, and be filled so I can go out and be useful to others.

Not everyone can find a whole room of her own, nor would everyone want to paint it pink, but I do think finding a space in your home and calling it your own is a valuable exercise. If it's a corner in the family room or a special chair in the kitchen, or wherever you can plant yourself for a little "me" time, try it and see if it's good for your soul.

When you live in a home filled with boys and their testosterone, female connection is hard to come by, but make it a priority, because it's important to helping you thrive.

A girls' getaway is always good medicine but not always possible. Sometimes a quick phone conversation with a friend helps. Maybe you can get away for a quick trip to a cute boutique filled with girly stuff like purses and make-up. Why not allow yourself a little self-indulgence, such as purchasing a pair of fuzzy pink slippers to wear around the house? Or maybe go someplace other than your boys' barbershop to get your hair cut and styled.

I've found that if I neglect the feminine side of myself, I'm not as good a wife and mother as I want to be. When I meet these needs, I feel balanced and fulfilled, and I know I'm easier to live with.

I encourage you to love your husband and boys with all your heart and to experience life with them, but also take time to nurture your feminine needs, because it will result in your becoming a happier, healthier, better wife, mother, sister, and friend.

Digging Deeper

Do you have a group of close friends? If not, there are still things you can do to build friendships. Some ideas I think are worth trying are to join a women's Bible study, start a women's hiking group, join a bunko group, or plan a girlfriend getaway with some of your friends.

Something to Think About

When you are busy and stressed, do you put friendships on the back burner?

If you answered yes, how can you incorporate spending time with friends even when you're stressed?

Do you have a space that is uniquely yours? If not, take an afternoon to create a space just for you.

Suggested Reading

Ruthellen Josselson, coauthor of *Best Friends: The Pleasures and Perils of Girls' and Women's Friendships*, wrote to me in an e-mail, "Friends are perhaps most important during times of stress, to understand, soothe, care, and generally be emotionally available. This is, in part, why it is so important for women to maintain their friendships even when they feel they can't make time for one single thing more."

Here are other scriptures on friendship: Proverbs 17:17; Proverbs 18:24; Proverbs 27:9; Ecclesiastes 4:9-10; John 15:13; 1 John 4:11.

8. The Superman Complex

By the grace given me I say to every one of you: Do not think of yourself more highly than you ought, but rather think of yourself with sober judgment, in accordance with the measure of faith God has given you.
—Romans 12:3

Suzie sat on the wooden bench at the playground, soaking up the warm afternoon sunshine and watching her four-year-old son, Walker, climb around on the purple play structure at her neighborhood park. Walker loved to climb, and Suzie, who was accustomed to seeing him up high in trees and other places that made some parents nervous, felt relaxed as Walker scrambled around like a monkey on the play set.

She glanced at him as he climbed the five-foot corkscrew ladder going up to the slide. She assumed he would take the step across the gap and slip down the slide as usual. Instead, she watched in terror as he spread his arms and dove off the top of the ladder. He landed hard on his belly. Suzie sprinted over to him, fearing he might have some serious injury.

"Walker, don't move. Mommy's here. Just calm down, Sweetie."

She gently turned him over as he gasped for air. He had knocked the wind out of himself and was having difficulty catching his breath. Another woman rushed over to help. Fortunately, she was a paramedic.

"I saw what happened. It looks like he knocked the wind out of himself pretty good." She smiled at Suzie as Walker let out a blood-curdling scream.

"I've seen kids take a fall like that and have some pretty serious internal bleeding. He seems okay, but if I were you I would take him to be checked by a doctor."

Suzie agreed but needed to calm him down first. She hugged Walker until he snuggled comfortably into her shoulder, then asked, "What were you doing?"

"I was being Superman." He sniffed and rubbed his watery eyes. "I thought I could fly," he said as he started whimpering.

Suzie took him to the doctor, who pronounced him healthy and advised him to not try flying like Superman again. Relieved yet baffled by Walker's belief that he could soar like Superman, Suzie took him home, determined to watch him more carefully in the future in case he decided to test his Superman abilities again.

Many boys are like Walker. They truly believe they can perform superhuman feats without getting hurt—and they're actually surprised when they learn they can't. Mark Moeller, an emergency room doctor in Boulder, Colorado, claims he frequently sees boys coming in with falls from stunts similar to Walker's. "Give a boy a cape, and don't be surprised if he thinks he can fly," he says. Dr. Moeller also emphasizes that boys not only do unwise stunts when they are young, but as they age they attempt dim-witted feats that cause more serious injuries. "They try to do crazy things such as jump from a rooftop onto a hammock below and end up with a broken pelvis, or jump over a burning sofa, lose their balance, and end up at a burn center with serious burns on both hands."

As parents, we try to teach our boys to have a realistic view of their human limitations. I hear myself repeating phrases such as "Don't run with that stick in your hand—you might fall" or "Put your helmet on in case you crash." I don't like to repeat these warnings over and over again, but over and over again my boys run with dagger-like sticks and jump onto their bikes without helmets. Of course, I hope they don't crash or fall, but I would like for my boys to realize that falling is a possibility and to take precautions—just in case. I do my best to remind them they're only human, but it's impossible to predict every scenario and always keep them out of harm's way.

For example, one day Jordan was jumping on the trampoline with a hammer in his hand. It never crossed my mind to tell the boys, "Don't jump on the tramp with a hammer in your hand. You might drop it onto your head." If I had, he might have escaped injury. Unfortunately, he came inside with a golf-ball sized lump and a deep cut on the top of his skull. I still don't really understand why he was jumping on the tramp with a hammer. It had something to do with trying to fix the basketball hoop the boys rigged up to hang over the net that surrounds our 15-foot round trampoline so they can do amazing spinning dunks and other acrobatic maneuvers.

You might assume that we rushed him to the emergency room, but we have come to consider ourselves experts in handling our boys' injuries. We've been to the emergency room so often that we're friends with the doctors—Dr. Moeller, for instance. So, instead of a panicked trip to the ER, Zane and I took a good look at his head. We decided stitches *might* be warranted, but no one would ever see the scar under his thick head of hair, so we gave him a bag of ice and sent him to the sofa to rest. We watched him for signs of a concussion for the next 24 hours and, after a couple of days, we were happy to see the cut healing fine without stitches.

Just as I couldn't foresee Jordan's dropping a hammer onto his head, I'm certain the mom of a young boy Dr. Moeller cared for one day never imagined her son would get himself into a very odd and painful predicament. As she tried on clothes in the changing room of a department store, her son grabbed a little jacket to try on. He must have become bored—as most boys do while shopping—and was holding the jacket over his head and zipping the zipper up and down. My guess is he was trying to make his own cape of some sort. She repeatedly asked him to stop playing with the zipper, but he didn't stop. Instead, he somehow managed to zip his eyelid into the zipper. It makes my eyes hurt just thinking about it.

The poor little guy was rushed to the emergency room by ambulance, with the jacket still attached to his eyelid. Dr. Moeller and another doctor faced an interesting dilemma. How do you unzip a boy's eyelid stuck in a jacket zipper? Word of this unusual situation spread throughout the hospital as various doctors, nurses, security guards, and even custodians came to watch how they were going to extract the eyelid from the jacket. Eventually, after sedating the young boy, they carefully took apart the zipper. The boy ended up with a railroad track-shaped bruise on his eyelid but nothing more serious.

Can you imagine the mom in the dressing room telling her son to stop playing with the zipper because "you might get your eyelid stuck in it"? I'm sure she never imagined that could even happen! Even if she did say something along those lines, I'm sure anyone within hearing distance—including her son—would have laughed. He was just having a little innocent fun to pass the time waiting for his mom.

As I considered boys' tendencies to believe they're indestructible, I decided it would be interesting to see if there's a difference between the number of boys who make trips to the emergency rooms and the number of girls who end up in emergency rooms. I was certain boys would outnumber girls by a huge margin. However, I was surprised to find out just the opposite. According to the most recent statistics gathered by the Centers for Disease Control in a one-year study, girls visited the ER 62,109 times, while boys lagged behind at 53,213 times.[1] Boys outnumbered girls by a couple thousand in the age group of 15 and under, but in all the other age groups, ranging from birth to 75 years and over, females frequented the ER more than males.

Dr. Moeller didn't find this very surprising. He said it seems to be about 50-50 in the patients he sees. However, he did say boys come in with more serious injuries such as broken bones rather than sprains and cuts needing stitches.

As we talked, I realized that this statistic did make sense after all. As parents of boys, Zane and I don't hurry into the ER anymore, as I mentioned previously. We first make sure it's an injury that really warrants medical attention. Sometimes we even wait a day or two, like once when Jake broke his hand. His knuckle swelled up, but because he was able to move his fingers, I sent him to school the following day.

When I picked him up, the top of his hand was still very swollen. We went to the doctor, had it X-rayed, and found it was indeed broken. I felt terrible that I had sent him to school with a broken bone. But in the end he was okay, and our doctor bill wasn't as high as it would have been if we had visited the emergency room.

"Do not think of yourself more highly than you ought, but rather think of yourself with sober judgment" (Romans 12:3). This scripture reminds me to teach our boys an important character trait: humility. Most parents today don't have trouble building up their boys. In fact, it seems to me children are being over-praised for simple things like brushing their teeth or are given huge trophies for every little team they're on. As a generation of parents who are proficient at praise, we might actually be adding to our boys' supermen complexes, magnifying their own puffed-up ideas of themselves. I believe boys need a dose of humility every once in a while. As parents, we need to keep diligent in reminding our boys that they're not superhuman.

Unfortunately, they don't always listen and have to learn through experience, as did the boy in a photo someone sent me an Internet link to. The photo is titled "Never Run with a Fork!" It's a shocking picture of a young boy sitting on his mom's lap with all four prongs of a metal fork poking through his swollen nose. If you must see this unpleasant picture, go to YouTube and search "kid, nose, fork." If your boys don't listen to you the next time you tell them not to run with a fork, show them this picture. I guarantee they will never-ever run with a fork again, even if they're wearing capes!

Do your boys a favor and don't grow weary of reminding them of their human limitations. Of course, you should keep praising them, but remember that it's okay to balance praise with reminders like "Don't forget your helmet," "Don't put that balloon in your mouth," "Don't dive off that ladder head first," "Don't jump on the trampoline with a hammer," and even "Stop playing with that zipper—you might get your eyelid stuck in it!" If it teaches your son to pause and think soberly about the possibilities, then just say it.

Digging Deeper

Write down something crazy you did as a child that caused you to end up in the emergency room.

On a scale of 1 to 10, 1 being very low and 10 being very high, how would you rate your son's self-confidence?

If you feel your son has low-self esteem, what can you do to help him be more confident? Or if you feel your son thinks too highly of himself, how can you help him develop humility?

How would you describe the difference between being self-confident and being God-confident?

9. Boys Are a Blast

I have come that they may have life, and have it to the full.
—John 10:10

Josh and his buddy concocted the perfect plan.

They snuck firecrackers in their backpacks to camp to play a practical joke on the girls. When the girls had a small-group gathering, the two boys stealthily crept into the bathroom near the girls' meeting room. Their plan was to throw a Black Cat firecracker into the toilet to create an earsplitting blast, complete with water works—water splashing up out of the toilet like "Old Faithful," the geyser at Yellowstone National Park. A Black Cat is a small firecracker that doesn't do much except make a fairly loud noise. They had practiced this stunt in our backyard, throwing the fireworks into a metal bucket filled with water, successfully causing a loud bang and a big splash. They figured throwing it in water was an excellent idea, because it would prevent an unwanted fire.

Their goal was to scare the living daylights out of the girls.

They stood over the toilet, lit the firecracker, and dropped it into the ceramic bowl. The Black Cat exploded all right—and so did the entire toilet. The ceramic shattered, and gallons of water spilled out onto the floor.

The college-aged counselor, who was a tough ROTC member, came flying into the bathroom to discover the boys staring at him with shell-shocked faces, still holding the matches in their hands. He gave them an earful and sent them to their rooms until he could talk with the camp director about what to do.

Meanwhile, the plumber came, patched up the damage, and replaced the toilet for a mere $800.00. Did I mention that this was very late at night? He pointed out how lucky they were they hadn't flushed the firecracker down the toilet because it would have been a huge mess, possibly bursting the underground pipes and requiring an incredible amount of time and money to repair.

I read a short story in a book called *Up to No Good: The Rascally Things Boys Do As Told By Perfectly Decent Grown Men*, a fun book filled with stories from men about the bad things they did when they were kids.

Dave from Washington tells his story:

A friend and I found a coffee can of gasoline in the garage and decided to pour some down a manhole, light it, and see what would happen. We popped the manhole open, poured some gas in, and replaced the cover so that it was ajar. We kept throwing matches down but nothing happened, so we poured all the gas in. Finally there was a noise like a jet engine starting up, and then a big BOOM! The manhole cover flew up and a flame shot up about fifteen feet in the air. The ground was rumbling like an earthquake, and the manhole cover crashed about twelve feet away in the neighbor's driveway. What happened was the gas ran down the sewer lines for a block or so and vaporized with all the methane in there, and blew up all our neighbors' toilets. I'm a plumber now; that's how I know exactly what happened.[1]

When we got the call from Josh, who said, "Mom, Dad— I blew up a toilet," we felt terrible, and so did he. He didn't intend to damage the property. Fortunately, the camp director, who is a close friend, wasn't too angry. In fact, I think he had a good chuckle about it as he imagined the surprised looks on their faces when the whole toilet blew up. He did require them to come up to camp later in the summer and do hard physical labor for four days to help pay for the damages.

As I've told others about Josh's experience, it inevitably brings to peoples' minds other stories they've heard about boys and fireworks and explosions. I don't know what it is, but the male attraction to explosives must be something genetic.

When boys and fireworks—or any type of explosives— come together, I believe the male brain completely stops working logically. It's like a lapse into insanity, causing the male creature to do something utterly out of character, usually somewhat stupid. I could tell many stories about my boys and fireworks, but if you're reading this book, you have boys and you probably have your own.

Boys love loud noises, bright flashing colors, the thrill of setting something on fire, and the after-effects, such as scaring innocent victims or lingering lines of smelly smoke. They also get a total kick out of blowing something to smithereens such as an apple, a Barbie doll, or some other random item.

I asked Zane why he thinks boys are so attracted to fireworks, and he said, "When a boy sees the fireball and hears the sound that comes from the explosion, he has a surge of adrenalin. He begins to fantasize about how he can get this adrenalin rush again. Then he acts on his illogical impulses to create and recreate new opportunities to fill his senses and startle his friends, neighbors, and sometimes enemies."

According to Zane, the boy then uses his creative abilities to regularly invent new ways to employ fireworks and continue to get that rush, such as turning a pop bottle rocket into a jetpack taped to the back of a grasshopper or creating a *real* minefield for his green plastic army men in the sandbox. Zane does feel there's something genetic about this fascination because, even with the high risk of injuring grasshoppers, burning off eyelashes, burning fields, and angering neighbors, this interest continues from generation to generation. "Mostly," Zane says, "it's just *fun!*"—not that he ever did any of those things *himself,* he rushes to assure me.

Whatever the reason, I've realized that I can't change my boys' fascination with fireworks, so I've had to change my perception. I've decided to look at this area in their lives with a positive attitude. The Fourth of July is a big deal at our house. In fact, it's the boys' second favorite holiday, following Christmas. April Fool's Day ranks a close third place. The moment the boys see the fireworks stands popping up around the outskirts of town, they empty their piggy banks, convince me to take them to the tents, and then purchase as many firecrackers as they can afford. Zane and I emphasize the importance of safety, such as always having a working hose nearby, and then let them go for it.

I've chosen to accept their love for fireworks because it typifies something I truly believe—boys are a blast! They know how to have a good time, and they have taught me by their enthusiasm of the simple pleasure of enjoying fire-crackers, how to enjoy life, live it to the full, and make every day a celebration—complete with a fireworks display.

In *The Mommy Diaries: Finding Yourself in the Daily Adventures,* Cathy Penshorn writes about how her boys taught her to push herself into new places and new experiences. She shares an example of their encouraging her to go down a high waterslide, something she felt terrified to do. She preferred to sit poolside and watch. Finally, after much persuading, she tried it. She writes,

And you know what happened? I learned that tall waterslides are fun, that stretching isn't so bad, and that living a little more on the wild side with the guys can rejuvenate me in ways that demurely sitting by the pool with a book just can't do.[2]

For dads, boys can reawaken that zest for life they had when they were young. Zane has just as much fun as the boys when they pull out the fireworks. He's been known to run through the neighborhood and light fireworks on neighbors' front porches with the boys, laughing hysterically as the occupants find a surprise when they open their front doors. In truth, every year around the Fourth of July, several neighborhood dads reignite their ongoing rivalry as they become intent on attacking one another's homes at unexpected moments.

As moms, most of us just laugh about this tradition, but we are occasionally spotted lurking alongside the boys, wearing all black and carrying a bag with an array of explosives. We're much less likely than the guys to get caught. We keep our brains intact and run as far away as possible—unlike the males, who lose all rational thought because they have to stay close enough to hear the explosion and see the surprised faces of their targets.

Raising boys has caused me to experience and enjoy life in a way I never would have known except for their influence. I probably wouldn't have noticed the cool bugs with the green-and-orange spotted wings that exist in our yard. I probably wouldn't have been motivated to go on night hikes and look for bats that sleep under the bridge nearby. I probably wouldn't have signed up to play in an adult soccer game against the boys just for fun. I certainly wouldn't have jumped off a 40-foot cliff into a freezing cold lake without their encouragement. I *never* would have pet a tarantula or wrapped a snake around my wrist. By no means would I have thought to wrap a ping-pong ball with foil and light it on fire to create a homemade smoke bomb (I'm sure the fumes were not healthy.) But now I've done all these things and more. And I can't say I regret it.

Thanks to my boys, I believe God has made Jesus' words ring true in my life: "I have come that they may have life, and have it to the full" (John 10:10). My life feels so full and so alive that I'm grateful beyond words for my boys and the experiences they've brought into my world.

Digging Deeper

What's something you're grateful you have experienced because of your boys' influence in your life?

Do you feel you encourage your boys to "live life to the full" or not? If not, how can you encourage this in their lives?

Ask a science teacher for a safe activity to create a small explosion or a firework. Do it with your boys.

Suggested Reading

Read these Scripture references related to experiencing an abundant life: Psalm 16:11; Psalm 145:1-7; Romans 15:13.

10. Sons of Thunder Mother/ Father Syndrome

The mother of Zebedee's sons came to Jesus with her sons and,
kneeling down, asked a favor of him. "What is it you want?" he asked.
She said, "Grant that one of these two sons of mine may sit
at your right and the other at your left in your kingdom."
"You don't know what you are asking," Jesus said to them.
—Matthew 20:20-22

Liz watched her 15-year-old son, Andy, sit on the bench for the third football game in a row. He had sprained his wrist a few weeks earlier, but it was fine now. He stared at the ground and dug with his muddy cleats into the grass. He occasionally glanced up to watch the game and spoke a few words to the kid sitting next to him. It broke her heart to watch him sit on the sidelines when, previously, he was a starter for the JV team. *Shoot—this is ridiculous,* she thought. *It's not his fault he was injured. He worked so hard to earn a starting spot on this team. I'm calling the varsity coach and see what he thinks Andy should do.*

When she got home, Liz snatched up the phone and called the coach, who also happened to be a friend of hers. After she explained her son's situation to him, she inquired, "He doesn't want to sit on the bench the rest of the season. What do you think Andy should do?"

"Liz, I'll be honest," he responded. "I really don't think it's up to parents to talk to coaches. It's up to the kids to communicate with them. You tell Andy to go talk to his coach."

The coach's sharp words stung, but Liz knew he was right. After she hung up the phone, she realized she had tried to interfere in her son's circumstances, and it wasn't her place to do that. The best thing for her son was for him to learn to speak up for himself. By meddling in this situation, not only had she embarrassed herself, but, if her son knew what she had done, he would have felt tremendously embarrassed too.

Liz, whose two boys are now grown, married, and starting their own families, said, "It was my tendency to try to fix my boys' problems. But I eventually learned that wasn't always the best for them. As a parent I wanted to protect my kids, but when they got to a place where I didn't—or couldn't—step in and protect them, that's when they learned tools for life."

One of her sons went into the military after high school. In Baghdad he served as a gunner on a Humvee, one of the most dangerous jobs. While he was away, Liz feared for his life, but she put into practice what she had learned about parenting: she couldn't fix everything and had to trust her son and his situation to a greater problem-solver—God Almighty.

She came to the Lord daily on his behalf, and he did come home safely. During his stint in Baghdad he had to put into practice the life tools he had learned as a teenager, such as perseverance, determination, and his own faith in God.

Many parents, including me, have a serious case of what I call the "Sons of Thunder Mother [or Father] Syndrome," which I define as attempting to manipulate our children's circumstances to result in the outcome we think is the best for them.

James and John were nicknamed the "Sons of Thunder" because of a scene in the Bible in which they became livid with the people of a town who refused to welcome Jesus. They asked if they should call down fire and obliterate the place (Luke 9:24). These two young men were overly confident, reactive, and swift to become angry. My guess is that they were pretty used to getting what they asked for in life. Perhaps their mother and father were quick to meet their needs, fix their problems, strategize, network, and manipulate their circumstances for their benefit, which can lead to very self-absorbed children.

Anyway, their well-meaning, although possibly meddling, mother knelt before Jesus and made a request on their behalf. She asked that they each be given a place on either side of Him, a place she thought would guarantee incredible opportunities for them when Jesus set up His kingdom. Although well-intended, she was trying to manipulate her sons' circumstances to help them achieve what she thought would be best for them. And Jesus reprimanded her. He told her they would drink from His cup, but she really didn't understand what she was asking. Drinking from His cup was not a pleasant sip of ice cold root beer served up in a frosty mug. It meant suffering and dying for a greater cause, for the benefit of others rather than for themselves.

At the time of their mother's request, the boys hadn't yet learned humility and the practice of putting others' desires before their own. They needed to grow deeper in their understanding of who Jesus was and what He came to do before they had the strength to accomplish what Jesus had called them to do. Jesus knew their futures, and He knew their mother had to let go of her idea of what their lives should look like.

James and John eventually died for their faith. James was the first of all the disciples to be killed. Herod beheaded him in 44 A.D. John was exiled to years of hard labor on the Isle of Patmos, where he died of old age. He was the last disciple to die. These brothers started off as feisty young men determined to help Jesus take over. In their mother's wildest dreams she probably could never have imagined the incredible influence her sons would have on the entire world, including future generations, in spreading the Good News Jesus brought to the earth—Jesus, the Son of God, who died, rose from the dead, and offered total forgiveness of sin and life after death just through believing in Him.

As I kneel before God on behalf of my boys, I sometimes am like the Sons of Thunder's mother. I want God to grant my wishes for them, to see them become all I think they should be. But often He has something else in mind. I strongly believe we should always kneel before Jesus and ask Him for blessings on their behalf. But, and this is the hard part, we need to trust and leave the outcome to Him.

On a more practical, daily basis, we have to figure out when, as parents, we need to step up and step in on behalf of our boys and when we should not meddle in their specific situations.

I don't think a simple answer exists to these questions. Rather, each individual family must make decisions based on each individual circumstance. However, there's one important question I challenge you to ask yourself when faced with this dilemma: "What are my motivations?"

My Motivations

Be honest with yourself. If your motivations are similar to those of the mother of James and John, to selfishly seek opportunity for your boys leading to fame, power, or success (selfish because their success makes us, their parents, look successful too), then you might want to hold your tongue. If you see it as a time to protect your boys from harm, then by all means, jump in. If you see an opportunity for them to advocate for themselves, then stay out of the way. If you see a chance to teach them and allow them to grow in faith and character, do whatever you can do to achieve that end.

Here's another suggestion: If faced with the choice of intervening on your son's behalf or not, follow the simple rule of what to do when your hair or clothes catch on fire: Stop, drop, and roll.

Stop: Stop yourself from taking immediate action. Reactive behavior often adds fuel to the fire, complicating the situation and leading to later regrets.

Drop: Drop to your knees and pray for wisdom.

Roll: After taking time to gain a healthy perspective,

which includes examining your own motives, start rolling forward with what you think you should do. It's always a good idea to talk to others and gather advice. Talk to your spouse, a good friend, a pastor, a counselor, or anyone else who can give you valuable counsel. Then take the appropriate action or no action, depending on what you prayerfully decide.

As I've written this chapter, I'm again being challenged with the exact issue I'm writing about. I've been tempted to e-mail one of Josh's high school math teachers. Josh is struggling in this class, and I want to ask what *we* can do to help him. For the last several days I've even brought up the teacher's e-mail to send him a note and then stopped. I've prayed about it, and after discussions with Zane, concluded it's Josh's responsibility to talk to this teacher—to advocate for himself.

I'm trying hard not to meddle in this situation, and I'm watching to see what Josh learns. I've realized that even if he fails, sometimes failure is the best place to learn and grow in character.

Abraham Lincoln experienced many failures, including failing in business, suffering a nervous breakdown a year after his sweetheart died, and losing many elections before becoming one of the United States' most famous presidents. Michael Jordan was cut from his high school varsity basketball team when he was a sophomore. He said this only motivated him to work harder. He practiced several hours each day, and when he felt tired, he closed his eyes and saw the list of players without his name in the list, and that spurred him to keep practicing. The apostle Paul endured all sorts of difficulties, including beatings, jail, a shipwreck, and even a snake bite, but he never gave up.

You never read about these men's parents stepping in and trying to change their circumstances. These men figured these things out on their own, in their own time and through their own journeys. During their challenges they developed persistence, determination, motivation, and all sorts of other positive qualities to help them through life.

Next time your son is in the midst of a situation that may or may not need your interference, remember to stop, drop, and roll, and see how he grows in the midst of life's challenges.

Digging Deeper

Describe a current or recent situation in which you find yourself facing the dilemma of whether or not to intervene on behalf of your son.

Stop.
Drop. Pray. Write your prayer here:

Roll.
Write out your motives—and be honest with yourself.

Seek advice from others, and write their advice here:

Write out what you're going to do—or not do—and what you hope your son learns through this specific situation.

Suggested Reading

Here are a few scriptures about examining your heart and mind: Psalm 51:10; Matthew 5:8; Mark 12:30-31; Romans 12:2; 2 Timothy 2:22.

11. Speaking of Love

Dear children, let us not love with words or tongue
but with actions and in truth.
—1 John 3:18

"In fifth grade I developed this major crush on a sixth-grader named Wendy," says John from Connecticut in *Up to No Good: The Rascally Things Boys Do.* "She always had the prettiest face and the nicest smile; everybody thought so. So I started kissing rocks and throwing them at her." [1]

John's actions are not that surprising if you're around boys most of your day. When it comes to expressing love, boys seem to have the tendency to *do* something rather than *say* something.

For example, one day when Jake was eight years old, I had some time alone with him. I asked him, "It's just you and me, buddy. What do you want to do this afternoon?"

"I want to go fishing," he replied.

I did say he could pick whatever he wanted to do.

"Umm, well, okay. But I don't know where everything is, do you?"

113

"Yeah, it's all in the back corner of the garage. I know where Daddy keeps all his fishing stuff." Zane is an avid fly-fisherman with enough gear to take several families on a fishing excursion.

"Jake, I have no idea what fly to use, or even how to tie it on the line. Are you sure you want *me* to take you fishing? Maybe Daddy could take you soon."

"No, Mom. I know what to do." Underneath his red, worn baseball cap, his blond curly hair stuck out, and his chocolate brown eyes lit up with confidence.

"All right," I said hesitantly.

Jake gathered up the gear he needed, and we drove to a kids' fishing pond not far from our house. We unloaded, and Jake started fishing. I sat down on the ground, leaned against a tree, and watched. Jake cast his fly into the pond, concentrating intently as he gently pulled the line toward him through the water and then cast again.

Within 10 minutes he had hooked his first fish. He reeled it in, quickly took the hook out of its mouth, and tenderly set it back in the water to swim away. Thrilled, he went at it again. He kept catching fish. People started stopping along the path to watch him and talk to him. Then out of the blue he announced, "Mom, the next fish I catch you can reel in."

I knew this was Jake's way of showing me he loved me. Giving up the thrill of catching the "big one" and offering his mom the chance to experience that thrill was a huge sacrifice for him. He wanted to give me something, and in that moment that was the biggest and best thing he could give me to show he loved me.

Sure enough, he caught another one. He hollered at me to come and reel it in. I jumped up, and he handed me the rod and instructed me how to keep the tip up and gently pull the fish in. It wasn't a very big one, but in my heart I felt as if I had experienced the catch of a lifetime.

That's an awesome thing about boys. They may not be adept at verbalizing their love, but it comes pretty naturally for them to show love with actions, to "not love with words or tongue but with actions and in truth" (1 John 3:18).

Love in Action

Many times, actions do speak louder than words. As Christians, a huge factor in living out our faith is doing acts of love toward others. Teaching boys to do this isn't that hard, because they're naturally doers.

Zane models this "love in action" attitude amazingly well to our family. He recently wrote his own personal mission statement, and one of his goals is to do acts of love toward others. And he does them. Whenever a big snowstorm hits, he's out before the sun rises shoveling our elderly neighbors' sidewalks. He tries to get the boys to help, but they're not always eager to venture out in the freezing temperatures to shovel snow when they still need to get ready for school and they know they won't get paid. But I have occasionally seen them doing thoughtful deeds for our neighbors without being asked and without expecting anything in return.

One winter we had mounds of snow and ice piled up. One of our neighbors, who's 85 years old and had just spent several weeks in the hospital due to a broken hip, had received a complaint from the city about the dangerous ice on the sidewalk in front of his home. He needed help getting rid of it. So on a Saturday our family, his family, and some other neighbors all helped break up the thick ice. We spent a couple of hours chipping away at the problem. After a while I realized Jordan wasn't around and wondered where he had gone. Eventually he came walking up the street with a shovel and ice pick.

"Where did you go?" I asked.

"I was helping Vinny and Priscilla," he said. They're our precious next-door neighbors who are in their 90s. "I felt bad we were all up here when they needed help too. I got rid of some of the ice on their doorstep."

I was happy Jordan had taken that initiative, but I realized he thought to do that because of the role model Zane is to our boys. Children do copy their parents' behaviors— good or bad. If we model loving others with actions and in truth, I believe this positive attitude will be contagious, and eventually our boys will do this too.

What Men Want

In Shaunti Feldhahn's book *For Women Only: What You Need to Know About the Inner Lives of Men*, she writes what she learned about men after interviewing more than 1,000 of them. She asked each an open-ended question: "What is the one thing you wish your wife or significant other knew, but you feel you can't explain to her or tell her?"

Through her survey, Feldhahn found that the number-one answer was "How much I love her."

Feldhahn was surprised at the overwhelming response to this question. She writes, "I was stunned. Here was a perfect opportunity for men to vent if they wanted to, or to share those things they wish their mates would work on. And yet, by far, the largest number of those responding—almost twice as many as the next highest response—chose to use the space to say that they wished their wife knew 'How much I really do love her.'"

She then concludes her book with "Men want to show us how much they love us, and they long for their women to understand what is going on inside, even though they sometimes can't explain it well."[2]

As parents of boys, we need to know this. When boys are young, it's not uncommon for them to attempt to show love through sometimes misunderstood actions, such as incessant wrestling with Mom, Dad, brothers, sisters, or pet dog, or kissing rocks and throwing them at the girl they have a crush on.

This reminds me of a story my friend Lisa told me involving her two young boys. Once when they were on a hike, they found a dead mouse on the trail. The boys begged her to bring it home, because they wanted to examine it. She agreed and used an extra doggie doo-doo bag in which to carry it. When they got home, she made both of the boys wear rubber gloves and gave them a lecture on the amount of disease a dead mouse carries. They were very careful as they handled the mouse.

Ty, her oldest, wanted to keep it in his bug collection box, so he ran inside to ask his dad if that was all right. My guess is that he didn't ask Mom, because she would have said no emphatically. Cole, her younger son, stood in the driveway, holding the dead mouse and anticipating his dad's answer. Ty came running out of the house and screamed, "Cole, Daddy said we can keep the mouse!"

"Yeah!" Cole hollered back. Lisa thought he was so excited that he might give Ty a big hug. Instead, he held the dead mouse up to his lips and gave it a huge kiss. Needless to say, she whisked Cole to the sink and washed his mouth and face with soap.

It struck me that Cole was so overwhelmed with joy—or so in love with the idea of keeping the dead mouse—that he had to do something, anything, to release that emotion. So he did what made sense to him: he kissed the dead mouse.

Another example of this is a situation my sister Jill, who has four boys, told me about. When her son Stephen was three years old, he loved the movie *Spy Kids*. Because the characters in the movie dressed in all black, he thought that was the coolest outfit ever. One day Jill came down the stairs dressed in all black. Stephen jumped out of his chair and met her halfway. "Mom, you're beautiful!" he exclaimed. He then latched onto her leg and would not let go. She dragged him down the stairs and around the house as he clung to her until she had to leave.

That's what I mean about boys and showing love. For them, like Cole and Stephen, it takes on a physical element, not just a verbal expression. They become so full of emotion that expressing it verbally just isn't enough; they have to do something physically to get the emotion out.

So next time your boy gets in trouble for throwing rocks at a little girl, wrestling with his best friend in class, tackling you from behind, or dumping out a pocket full of dead butterflies he collected for you—onto your clean kitchen countertop—don't be too hard on him; he's learning to love with actions and in truth. Recognize that it's his way of showing love.

Digging Deeper

Write down a memory of a time your son showed you love. Let him know this is a memory you cherish.

How can you model love in action to your son? Be specific about something you can do in the next two weeks and do it.

Ask your son to come up with an idea to show love to a neighbor and then do it.

Suggested Reading

Here are a few scriptures on showing love through actions: Matthew 5:16; Galatians 6:9; Ephesians 2:8-10; 1 Timothy 6:18-19; Titus 3:4-8.

12. The Last Shall Be First

Do nothing out of selfish ambition or vain conceit, but in humility consider others better than yourselves. Each of you should look not only to your own interests, but also to the interests of others.
—Philippians 2:3-4

We recently took a vacation with my extended family—18 of us—to Mexico. Just as our plane landed on the runway back at Denver International Airport, Josh leaned over my seat and said, "Mom, we're going to be the first ones to baggage claim, so be ready to run when we get off this plane."

The boys' goal was to beat my two sisters' families and my parents. Truthfully, my boys wanted to outrun everyone on the charter flight.

I didn't really understand.

I am not going to run through the airport, I determined. Besides, I felt embarrassed. I didn't want to attract attention by sprinting past all these weary travelers.

"Come on, Mom," all the boys pleaded, including Zane. Then Jake, my 11-year-old, added, "You're going to be the weak link!"

I had heard that before.

A couple of years earlier some friends of ours were selected to be on *Trading Spaces: Family*. It's a reality TV program in which two sets of neighbors spend two days redecorating a room in each other's homes using a budget of $1,000. Our friends were thrilled. The only problem was that they're a family of five, and only four family members were allowed to participate. After much dialogue, they decided the dad would be the one to step out of the show. It was a hard decision, but all three kids and the mom wanted to do it. So the unselfish dad relinquished his place and put his kids and wife's desires ahead of his own.

Watching our friends be a part of this reality program caused our family to talk about what it would be like to do something like this. We decided that the best show for us to be on, and have an actual shot at winning, would be *The Amazing Race: Family Edition*. In this program, family members race around the world trying to be the first to arrive at specific destinations. The winners receive a large cash prize.

Based on our traveling experiences and an uncanny ability to get someplace first, we would be great contestants for this show. Even without my participation, my boys did win the family race through the airport. They just grabbed my stuff for me and kept going. Never mind that the other members of my extended family didn't even realize it was a race. And almost every other time we've traveled, we've been first in line, first to get our bags out the airport door, first to get on the shuttle, first to get a rental car, and so on. We're not ones to wait patiently in lines and allow the weak and elderly to go ahead of us.

After we decided that we would be formidable contestants, I made the mistake of asking a dumb question: "If only four of us could be on *The Amazing Race*, who would we kick out?"

During a moment of awkward silence, Zane and the three boys all looked around at each other. No one wanted to be the bearer of bad news. Finally, Jake spoke up, "Mom, you're the weak link." They all nodded in agreement.

The truth hurts sometimes. I don't possess the drive it takes to ruthlessly win a competition like *The Amazing Race*, but the boys do. As a female, I am more sensitive and aware of people's feelings. I know it annoys people when we zoom past them to get in line first, and I don't like to make people feel irritated. The boys are just focused on the race, a bit clueless about others' feelings. Their goal is to be first, and they usually are, regardless of how it makes others feel.

I believe this "me first" attitude boils down to an innate selfishness. From a very early age, our boys have wanted to be first always: first in any line, first to eat, first in track and field day in any event, first to run in the front door after an outing, first down the ski run, first to roll up the car window, and first in _____ (fill in the blank).

Don't get me wrong: I'm not saying I'm not selfish too. In fact, my motivations for not racing through the airport when we returned home from Mexico were also selfish. I really cared more about what others thought of me and my boys than I did about helping others and letting folks go in front of me.

Teaching boys—or any human beings—the practice of putting the needs of others ahead of their own goes against their natural tendency. It's a huge parenting challenge, because we have to exhibit an unselfish attitude in our own daily lives. The Bible tells us, "Do *nothing* out of selfish ambition or vain conceit, but in humility consider others better than yourselves. Each of you should look not only to your own interests, but also to the interests of others" (Philippians 2:3-4, emphasis added). But how can we, as parents of boys, do nothing out of selfish ambition or vain conceit? It's a daily battle, but just recognizing it and examining our motives will lead to the next step of denying ourselves and putting others' needs first.

A Lesson in Unselfishness

A story in the Bible describes one tough lesson on selfishness when David's eyes were opened wide to this particular sin in his life.

At one point, he was hiding in a cave while battles raged around him. Men fought valiantly until they were so weary they could barely cling to their swords, and the Lord granted them victories in battles against incredible odds. Three mighty men, who were singled out due to their devotion to David and God, came to visit David in his cave. Meanwhile, their enemies, the Philistines, were camping in Bethlehem not far from David's hideout.

David suddenly had a craving for water from Bethlehem's well and said, "'Oh, that someone would get me a drink of water from the well near the gate of Bethlehem!' So the three mighty men broke through the Philistine lines, drew water from the well near the gate of Bethlehem and carried it back to David" (2 Samuel 23:15-16).

Something clicked in David's conscience. He knew he had said something selfish, and three men had almost died to bring him a drink of water. "He refused to drink it; instead, he poured it out before the LORD. 'Far be it from me, O LORD, to do this!' he said. 'Is it not the blood of men who went at the risk of their lives?' And David would not drink it" (2 Samuel 23:16-17).

He realized the men's gift was too great a sacrifice for him to enjoy it. I think he poured out the water partly as a statement to them and to the Lord of his repentance for being so egocentric and to set an example of denying himself. He poured this gift "out before the LORD" rather than selfishly satisfy his own thirst.

In *My Utmost for His Highest* Oswald Chambers writes about this story in his September 3 entry:

Love has to get to its transfiguration point of being poured out unto the Lord. If you have become bitter and sour, it is because when God gave you a blessing you clutched it for yourself; whereas if you had poured it out unto the Lord, you would have been the sweetest person out of heaven. If you are always taking blessings to yourself and never learn to pour out anything unto the Lord, other people do not get their horizon enlarged through you.[1]

Who are those other people in your life? Perhaps they are your own sons. Through denying yourself and meeting others' needs, you're showing your boys an excellent way to live. You're enlarging your boys' horizons, showing them that you're concerned not only for your own interests but also for the interests of others.

A Real-life Servant

I recently read an inspirational story about a real, live, modern-day saint, an unselfish, serving man named Albert Lexie. He's a 64-year old developmentally disabled gentleman who has given more than $113,000 to the Children's Hospital of Pittsburgh to help critically ill kids receive the medical care they need regardless of the family's ability to pay.

When Albert was 15 years old, he made a shoeshine box in high school shop class. Once a week for years he took his little box to the Children's Hospital and shined doctors' shoes. One day he saw an annual telethon asking for money for the hospital to help sick children pay their bills. He changed into his best clothes, went to his bank, withdrew his entire life savings of $750, and donated it all—every penny.

Since that day in 1981, every Tuesday and Thursday Albert is found at the hospital shining shoes. He charges $3 a shine and then gives all his tips to the hospital. He usually earns $10,000 a year for himself and gives $10,000 away.

In an interview, CBS News Correspondent Lee Cowan asked, "Why do you do this, Albert?"

"Because I love the kids very much—I think they're very special," he answered.

"You really care about them, don't you?" Cowan remarked.

"Sure do," Albert said.

"You don't even know them," noted Cowan.

"[I] don't know them, but [I] still love them," Albert explained. "That's why God put [me] here."[2]

Albert has won many prestigious awards for his selfless

service and positive impact on society. He's been written about in *Reader's Digest, People,* and other magazines and books and has even appeared on *The Oprah Winfrey Show.* But he never boasts of these things. He just keeps shining shoes. His life is not about being a celebrity; it's about being a servant. Day after day he gets on his knees, humbly shines shoes, and then generously gives to help sick children. He lives to serve.

I share this story because I want you to tell your sons about this extraordinary man. I believe in the power of storytelling. Jesus frequently told stories to make a spiritual point, and most of us remember His stories. I believe your son will remember a story like this and file it away somewhere in his brain. The next time he sees an obviously sick child or a homeless person without a coat, he might remember Albert Lexie and be moved to place his own needs aside and do something to help someone else.

I have a friend who recently shared Albert's story with her teenage son one Saturday night when they went out for dinner. It was a week before Christmas—a time when most kids, especially teenagers, are quite selfish, thinking mostly about what they want. The mother and son spent a little time talking about Christmas. Her son mentioned he had saved some money and planned to combine it with the money he expected from his grandparents to buy new ski goggles. When his mom shared the story about Albert, her son listened. The teen remarked, "Wow—$10,000 isn't much to live on, and to give that same amount away is incredible." The story seemed to touch a tender place in the teen's heart.

The next morning they went to church. During the service they saw a slideshow of people living in a refugee camp in Afghanistan. The pastor and a small group from the congregation had recently visited these people. The photos showed how the refugees dwelled in the mud under tarps held up with sticks. Temperatures in the winter dip below freezing, and most of the people have only flip-flops to wear, if any shoes at all. The church volunteers built a well and gave out winter clothes. Providing water and giving coats, hats, mittens, and boots, they impacted the refugees' lives in a big way.

The church decided to continue helping the refugees in this camp and asked for people to consider giving $25 as a Christmas gift to a family living there. That amount would feed a family for an entire month.

My friend's son quietly whispered, "I want to do that." He was motivated to give his money to help another family. Something clicked in his conscience that pushed his own needs to the background and placed someone else's needs first. He fed a family for a month, and that's no small thing.

Perhaps hearing about Albert Lexie, combined with seeing the real needs of others, played a role in impacting this teen's decision. We may never know exactly what caused his behavior, but it's worth trying with your own boys. Keep telling your boys stories, found in the Bible or in the news, about how other people's lives are changed for the better by someone who puts his or her own needs last and others' needs first.

Go for Second!

One of my favorite scenes in the movie *The Incredibles* is

near the end when the super boy, Dash, is running a race in a school track meet. His parents and siblings are in the bleachers cheering him on. The catch is that they don't want anyone to know of his super speed, but since he wants to participate in school sports like a normal kid, they allow him to join the team. He just has to hide his gift.

The race begins, and he holds back. His parents start yelling, "Run!" and "Pick up the pace!" He blasts forward, ahead of everyone. Then his dad yells, "Stop! Pull back a little bit!" And mom yells, "Go for second!" Dash nods, he understands, and with a smile on his face, he runs up to second place and proudly finishes second. Wouldn't that be a great motto in training boys to put others' needs ahead of their own?

Go for second, because God will reward those who put others first.

Digging Deeper

Tell your boys a story of a person you admire for his or her unselfishisness.

Ask you son what it means to him to be unselfish.

Sign your family up for a mission trip. If you don't have a place in mind, ask your pastor for a suggestion.

Recommended Reading

Other suggested scriptures on servanthood: Mark 10:42-45; John 13:1-17.

13. Just Joking

Like a madman shooting firebrands or deadly arrows is a man who
deceives his neighbor and says, "I was only joking!"
—Proverbs 26:18-19

I stepped into the hallway and saw Zane lying on the floor outside the boys' bedroom. He was peeking into their room through the slit of the almost-closed door. He held something in his hand, but I couldn't make out what it was.

Before I had the chance to ask him what he was doing, he held his finger to his lips and whispered, "Shhh."

I crept up beside him, assuming he wanted me to not disturb the boys. He had just tucked them in for the night. I looked more closely and saw he was holding some fly-fishing line in his hand. It was looped around the door knob, then up and over the light on the ceiling of the boys' room. As I followed its trail, I saw, tied to the other end, one of the boys' beanie babies, a purple lizard placed strategically in front of the boys' bunk bed.

Zane tugged on the fly line, and the beanie baby's head bobbed up and down. A few seconds later, Zane tugged on the line a little more vigorously, and the lizard's head bobbed up and down. Suddenly, the boys' eyes opened wide. Jordan, who was about four years old, started screaming, "It's moving! It's mooooving!"

Zane and I couldn't help ourselves. We burst out laughing. Even though it seemed cruel to scare little boys, it was hilarious! We rushed into their room and calmed them down. We showed them Zane's set-up. They both laughed, and for the next month whenever the boys had a friend over, they begged Zane to do that trick to their friends. He did. And we laughed some more.

For some families this might have crossed the line of appropriate joking, but for our family it was right in line with everyone's sense of humor. This is a story we retell over and over again. It's a fun memory, special to our family.

Practical jokes are a funny thing. Boys love to play pranks on each other or on just about anybody. Fooling someone else is something they love to do: doorbell ditching, making prank phone calls, putting a rubber band around the sink sprayer so it sprays whoever turns on the water, and whatever else they can think up. Joking around provides hours of entertainment. I think this has been a boy trait passed down through every generation. In *Up to No Good: The Rascally Things Boys Do*, one man tells of a prank he did with some buddies at school.

In seventh grade, the biology teacher had us dissect fetal pigs. My friends and I pocketed the snout of a pig and stuck it on the water fountain so that the water shot straight up out of the pig's nostrils. No one really noticed it until they were bent over just about to drink. The problem is that we wanted to stick around and see the results, but then we started laughing so hard that we got caught. We all got the paddle for that.[1]

The challenge for parents of boys is to keep those pranks from crossing the line of what's appropriate to what's not.

One night we came home to find the message light blinking on our phone. I retrieved the message. It was a creepy sounding, whispering voice, saying, "Jake, I'm going to kill you," over and over again. It sent a shiver up and down my spine. I saved the message and had Zane listen to it. We figured it was a joke, but it didn't feel right. Several recent attacks on innocent children had happened at schools around the country. These disturbing incidents had us all a little nervous about our kids' safety.

I checked the caller ID, and the boy who left the message hadn't been smart enough to realize we would immediately know the origin of the call. We phoned the boy's home and spoke with his dad. Fortunately, his dad took it seriously too. He talked to his son about the seriousness of threatening someone's life. He even had the boy meet with the principal at school and write an apology to our family.

This incident also provided a chance for Zane and me to talk with our boys about appropriate and inappropriate joking. We decided that if the person you're playing the joke on won't think it's funny, then it's probably not okay. We used doorbell ditching as an example. We have some neighbors who think it's funny and will play along, and others who get angry, march over, knock on our door, and complain. The boys know who is who. Learning to use good judgment in the area of teasing and joking with others is a fine art. It takes time and experience, but as boys mature, they figure it out—hopefully.

Zane and I do encourage the boys to joke around, because we're convinced God has a sense of humor. After all, we're made in His image (Genesis 1:27). He gave most of us funny bones.

The Bible even provides glimpses of God's sense of humor in some stories that are clever and comical, such as the story of Jonah, who gets swallowed up by a big fish and lives in its belly for three days until he gets burped up onto a beach. Or remember the story of Balaam and his talking donkey? "He was rebuked for his wrongdoing by a donkey—a beast without speech—who spoke with a man's voice and restrained the prophet's madness" (1 Peter 2:16). That must have been amusing for God. I wish I could have seen Balaam's face when his donkey opened his mouth and started talking.

Sometimes when we're just sitting around the house with nothing to do, we'll start surfing the Web for funny stuff. We've watched some very humorous pranks online. If you find a moment and need a good laugh, go to YouTube and search for "fake waterbed prank in a store." We've watched this one several times. We also enjoy watching funny movies and "America's Funniest Home Videos."

Enjoy goofing around with your boys. Let them play pranks on you. Joking around, without crossing lines of what's appropriate according to your family, can build lifelong memories and strong bonds. A family who laughs together stays together, or something like that.

Digging Deeper

Tell your boys about a practical joke you played on someone when you were a kid.

Rent a funny movie to watch together.

Plan a practical joke as a family, and do it. This is a good chance to talk about what's appropriate joking and what's not.

Do you think God has a sense of humor? Why or why not? Discuss this with your children.

Recommended Reading

Did you know there are almost 400 verses containing the word *joy* or *rejoice* in the Bible?

Here are a few: Ecclesiastes 3:4; 1 Chronicles 16:27-34; Psalm 5:11; Psalm 16:11; Acts 2:28; Philippians 4:4.

14. Behind Every Great Man Is— His Mother

Let us consider how we may spur one another
on toward love and good deeds.
—Hebrews 10:24

"What do you think you've learned about girls from me?" I asked Jordan and Jake one morning in the kitchen.

They both look at me somewhat confused. "What do you mean? You're not like a girl, you know? You're our mom," Jake said.

Then a light bulb went on in my brain: they don't think of me as a girl—I'm their mother. That's a whole different category. This bolstered my curiosity about what influence I have in their lives. I'm someone unique to them, someone who can have a powerful impact in their lives because of the particular God-given place I'm in as a mother of three boys.

I'm part of a bigger picture of raising tomorrow's men. These men will then bear the responsibility of fathering the next generation. I'm the primary female influence in their lives right now. How I act and treat them will have a significant impact on how they view females, how they live their lives, and who they become in this world. Wow—that's scary!

Overwhelmed by this thought, I decided to send out an e-mail to men I respect and ask them what influence their moms had in who they are today. These men hold a wide variety of positions in life. Including being dads, they're orthopedic surgeons, engineers, businessmen, firemen, software engineers, salesmen, entrepreneurs, and pastors.

Here are some of their responses to my question about how their moms positively influenced their lives:

She treated people with respect.

She taught me manners.

My mom encouraged Kool-Aid stands, selling seeds, and paper routes.

She consoled me when I came home from a little league game after the coach forgot to play me.

She modeled commitment. My mom was true to her word and stuck with my dad through ups and downs.

My mom loved my brother and me through our quirks.

She told me, "If you can't learn to like yourself, how can you expect anyone else to like you?" I've never been short on having a positive self-esteem.

She modeled serving others with acts of love.

She taught me to pray.

She never got sick and always took care of my brothers and me when we were sick.

She loved to laugh, and she smiled all the time.

Based on these responses, I developed several areas where Mom plays a special role in impacting her son's life.

Your role as a mother of boys in this life is one of the most important positions ever.

Moms help raise gentlemen. *Gentleman* is defined by Dictionary.com as "A well-mannered, considerate man with high standards of proper behavior." In a culture where manners seem to be growing obsolete, moms can continue training boys to be gentlemen. My mother used to read us rules out of a manner book when we were growing up. This drove my sisters and me crazy. Now I see the value in it. I've come to appreciate men who use good manners.

Women have come a long way in terms of being treated as equal to males, and that's good. But I still think women appreciate it when a man opens a door for her, lets her go ahead of him in line, offers her a seat on a crowded bus, carries her heavy bag, comes to the front door to pick her up for a date, doesn't use vulgar expressions or foul words, uses good table manners, and doesn't burp or do other gross things in her presence.

I realize I live with boys who don't view me as a typical girl because I'm their mom. They're comfortable with me, so comfortable that sometimes they treat me like one of the guys. They make unusual bodily noises around me or occasional crude statements. Some of those times I take the opportunity to say, "Guys, there's a girl in the room, me, and that's not appropriate." Sometimes they laugh it off; on occasion they say they're sorry. My hope is that I'm gently reminding them to be gentlemen, to remember to make women feel honored in their presence.

Moms help raise boys who are sensitive to others' feelings. Jake told me once that I was sensitive and emotional about my cooking. I guess I am. During the past 17 years I've spent countless hours thinking about what to feed the boys, walking up and down grocery aisles reading food labels and selecting ingredients to fill our fridge and pantry, and in the kitchen cooking. When I spend time creating a meal, I have expectations, such as everyone raving about my culinary skills. I envision our family sitting around the table, talking and laughing together, enjoying our meal. Nothing spoils that vision more than a kid looking at his food and saying something like, "Yuck!" or "Gross—what is it?" At those moments I let the boys know how this makes me feel. I've also learned to be flexible and not take it too personally if the boys don't like something I make.

I think the boys realize that because I'm a girl, I'm emotional and sensitive, not just about cooking but about a whole lot of other things as well. I do try to share my feelings with the boys and let them know if I'm hurt, proud, or touched by something they've said or done. I think this opens their eyes to the reality that girls have feelings and keeps on their radar how they make others feel with what they do or say.

Moms help teach boys communication skills. I touched on this a bit already in a previous chapter, "Communicating with the Caveman." As a reminder, Mom can use her female gift of gab to encourage boys to talk.

Moms teach boys to laugh. Humor is an essential life ingredient. I pray each of my boys marries a girl with a great sense of humor, someone who laughs often and can laugh at herself. My boys find plenty of things to laugh with me—or at me—about. For example, the night before my 20th high school reunion, I was playing tennis with Josh. I had bought a new dress to wear, whitened my teeth, and done other girly things to ensure I looked my best when I saw some of the people I hadn't seen for two decades. I didn't think twice about playing tennis the night before. I served the ball and ran toward the net to put away his return. Instead, I tripped over my own feet and did a face plant on the court, with my right cheek bone taking most of the impact. It hurt. I lay there for a moment and heard Josh say, "Mom, are you okay?" I looked at him, and it was obvious he was desperately trying to hold back an outburst of laughter. Then he added, "I won that point. My shot was in." I started laughing, and then we both laughed until our sides hurt. I attended my reunion sporting a nice big bruised cheek and black eye, causing people to wonder what in the world happened. We still crack up about that. Whenever I challenge Josh to a tennis match, he reminds me of my graceful fall.

Laughter makes life fun, and some of our best times as a family are laughing together. I hope my boys experience lots of laughter throughout their lives, especially with their future families.

Moms help build boys' self-esteem. Boys love to be watched. I can't begin to tell you the number of times a day one of my boys will want me to watch him. When they were young, they wanted me to see them slide down every slide, jump over every stream, or knock down every tower of building blocks. As they grow older, they still want me to watch them. I'm the designated photographer when we ski and they do tricks off jumps, tricks on rails, and ski through moguls. They holler at me to watch them jump off the high-dive, play ping-pong, teach our puppy new tricks, and almost anything and everything else. Even Zane likes me to watch him. Men like women's attention and approval, and as moms of boys, we're in a unique position to do this and do it well.

I see myself as the ultimate cheerleader. It's my job to watch them, to praise them, and to cheer them on. This builds their confidence, which can lead to their achieving their dreams.

One of my goals is to help my boys dream and dream *big* and then go after their dreams with confidence. In John and Helen Burns' book *What Dads Need to Know About Daughters/What Moms Need to Know About Sons*, they write, "A huge factor in determining who we become is the vision that others speak into our lives. The most potent words come from the most important people . . . no one is more important to a boy than Mom."[1]

I love that idea—speaking vision into our boys' lives. We impact who they become through how we see them and what we say to them. This affects how they view themselves in this world. As moms, we can cheer our boys on to great things, to believe positively about themselves, and to have confidence that when they leave our homes they know they can make a difference in the world.

Moms help raise physically and emotionally healthy boys. A Harvard University study found that 91 percent of college men who said they did not enjoy a close relationship with their moms developed coronary artery disease, hypertension, duodenal ulcers, and alcoholism by midlife. Only 45 percent of men who recalled warmth and closeness with their moms developed similar illnesses. James Dobson, in his book *Bringing Up Boys*, writes, "In short, the quality of early relationships between boys and their mothers is a powerful predictor of lifelong psychological and physical health."[2]

That's powerful. Our relationship with our sons affects them physically and emotionally. I always knew I was supposed to train them to eat well and exercise, to brush their teeth and change their underwear. But now I realize my relationship with my boys goes much deeper than an exterior physical health. Creating a bond, an emotionally close relationship to my boys, will help them be physically and emotionally healthy into adulthood.

To create this type of relationship, a mom must be intentional. Plan date nights. Tuck them into bed even when you're tired. Make dinner time special. Play with them. Talk to them. I want my boys to say things about me like the men I queried said about their moms. Be intentional in building a relationship that lasts a lifetime and leaves a positive imprint on your boys.

Moms help boys learn to love tenderly. The differences between men and women are vividly seen in the differences between moms and dads. Again, I'm speaking in generalizations, and this is not true about all parents, but typically the mom is tender and the dad is tough. Martin Luther King once spoke about the power of blending opposites, the ability "to be tough-minded and tenderhearted." I think God uses the differences between men and women in a powerful way in the family. The blending of these two characteristics, creating a healthy balance in a child, is amazing. For moms of boys, teaching tenderness helps balance their natural tendency for toughness.

Zane said one of his mom's positive influences in his life is how she consistently loved others through doing kind acts toward them. He especially remembers his mom bringing his grandpa into their home when he was diagnosed with cancer. She cooked a special diet for him, bathed him, kept him comfortable, and treated him with honor until he left this earth. This had a huge impact on Zane. He is committed to doing acts of kindness toward others, partly because he observed his mom doing this.

Moms teach boys what women think about men. You're the primary female influence in your son's life. He'll notice your view of men and transfer that into how he believes all women view men. If you as a female are critical and negative toward men, then your son will likely think that's how most women view men. How you treat your husband says volumes in a boy's mind about how women should treat men.

I once heard a comedian make a joke about marriage. He talked about how his quirks were so adorable when he was first married, like how he made those cute little whistling noises when he slept, or how he always organized his clothes in his closet according to color. Then 15 years later those cute quirks become probable cause.

People get irritated with each other about the dumbest things. One woman complained to me about how her husband squeezes the toothpaste tube from the middle rather than the end. Another woman griped about how her husband puts the toilet paper on wrong since he has the paper roll out from the bottom rather than the top. These women were seriously annoyed! How did they get to that point? My guess is that over the years they let these little idiosyncrasies become issues rather than laugh them off or let them go.

Be an example to your boys of a woman who loves and accepts her husband, quirks and all. Speak positively about and to your husband, and treat him with utmost respect. Husbands and wives should be accepting of one another's differences, and don't let petty points of disagreement grow into mountains of bitterness. Treat each other the way you hope your son and his wife will someday treat each other.

In Hebrews 10:24 the author writes, "Let us consider how we may spur one another on toward love and good deeds." I hope my life influences my boys to live a life loving others and spurs them on to good deeds.

Digging Deeper

Mother love is the fuel that enables a normal human being to do the impossible.
—Marion C. Garretty.

Do you believe you can have a significant impact on your sons? If yes, how? If no, why not?

Take a moment to consider how you can encourage your boys toward love and good deeds. Write something specific that you can do.

Of the different areas of influence you have on your sons that are mentioned in this chapter, which do you think you do well, and which do you need to improve on?

Are there other areas in which you feel you can have a positive influence on your son's life? What are they?

Recommended Reading

Read these Bible verses about a mother's influence on her son: Proverbs 23:15-16; Proverbs 23:25; Isaiah 66:13; Luke 1:46-55; 1 Thessalonians 2:6-8.

15. Let Go and Let Dad

All of you, clothe yourselves with humility toward one another, because,
"God opposes the proud but gives grace to the humble." Humble
yourselves, therefore, under God's mighty hand, that he may lift you up in
due time.
Cast all your anxiety on him because he cares for you.
—1 Peter 5:5-7

"Don't forget to give Alex his strep medicine three times a day," I heard my friend instruct her husband just before we left for a girls' weekend getaway. "Usually I give it to him at breakfast, lunch, and dinner."

"And give him yogurt with it so he doesn't get diarrhea," she added.

"Got it," her husband replied.

"And don't let them stay up too late. And no rough-housing."

"I know," he interrupted.

"And Tim wanted to do a sleepover with Ben Saturday night. I think that would be fun. Just don't let them watch a too-scary movie. Tim will have nightmares. Remember how scared he got watching *The Gremlins*?"

"Don't worry, I can handle it. I'm a big boy. Actually I'm their dad."

"Oh, yeah—sorry."

Sound familiar? For some reason moms want to instruct husbands on how to handle the kids rather than just let go and let dads be dads.

When our kids were small, it annoyed me when I heard a dad say, "I've got to baby-sit tonight." I used to remind these men that dads don't baby-sit—because they're dads. You *hire* a baby-sitter. You don't hire a father. Yet I found myself talking to Zane as I would a babysitter. I didn't mean for this to be negative; I truly thought I was just helping him, making it easier for him because I was with the kids more, and I was more familiar with their routines. At one point I finally realized I was taking away Zane's opportunity to be a dad and to use his own experiences, knowledge, and unique gifts to grow our boys into the men God designed them to be.

Now when I leave the boys home alone, I don't write lists, give Zane verbal instructions, or even pack the fridge with food as I used to do. When I leave, I kiss and hug them all goodbye and tell them to have fun.

Another reason women believe they know best about parenting is that they typically are the ones who read the parenting books. And women are more likely to spend hours discussing issues with friends, attending parenting seminars, and seeking counseling. So we assume we know best. It's important to apply what you learn but not to constantly correct your husband if he does things differently than the book you just read recommends or someone just advised you. Hopefully your husband is open to learning, too, but be sensitive to how you "help" him. It's tempting to try to control every aspect of what goes on in your home, including how your husband parents. Instead, pray for your husband, and loosen your grip on your children. Let him be a dad.

"Vacancy" Sign

For moms who have traveling husbands or husbands whose jobs require extensive hours out of the house, keep in mind your husband's need to feel needed when at home. Many women today are very independent and capable of handling multiple responsibilities, including running a household, overseeing children's homework, planning extracurricular activities, working, and raising children. They do it all well. Unfortunately, whether intended or not, this type of woman is sending a message to her husband that he's not needed at home.

In my Bible study I have several friends whose husbands have demanding jobs or travel extensively. These women said home feels like a hotel—a brief stop between business trips—for their husbands. At times, these women admitted, it was harder to parent when husbands came home, because the women were accustomed to parenting alone. One said her husband's sporadic involvement disrupted her working system.

Over time, the husbands expressed feeling left out and unneeded at home. One of my friends joked that she should put up a "Vacancy" sign in her home for her husband: a clear message that communicated to him, and reminded her, that a spot exists in her home where he is needed and that he's the only one who can fill that space. Not a bad idea. Whether you leave an actual sign up or make a concerted effort to include your husband when he's home, let him know he's needed.

Another of the girls in my study, a mother of two boys, sent me an e-mail about how she and her traveling husband found themselves living independent lives.

I thought I was supporting my husband by just letting him do his business thing and kind of leaving him out of the home front. He, too, would just step out of the disciplining role at home and let me do my thing in dealing with the boys. He said he did this because I was good at it and he felt he just got in the way. (Honestly, I kind of wanted it that way.) Basically, he didn't feel needed. I had it all under control at home.

What we did for years was dig these deep "ruts" in the road of life with a big mound in between us. In doing what we thought was supporting each other, we actually created this chasm of independence. We didn't need to communicate about anything because we each did what we were good at, and there was no crossover. My husband's traveling just made it even easier to function independently of him. We realized we had created some dysfunction in our parenting and needed to make some changes.

Now when he's home we work at activities that will engage all of us—board games, movies, or bowling. I also try to communicate with him what has happened while he's been gone. Sometimes I make a list of things to tell him about so that he can talk with the boys about their time while he was away. I also have the kids call him nightly while he's on the road so they feel connected.

Another friend whose husband travels often said she puts the phone on speaker mode and places it in the middle of the table during breakfast. They all chat with Dad throughout their meal. He hears them slurping their cereal, asking for juice, spilling their milk, and talking about their plans for the day. She said he loves this because he feels he's a part of their normal daily routine.

Be aware of the potential pattern in your own home of you being the supermom who takes care of everything on the home front, leaving your husband wondering where he fits in. It's crucial to let your husband know that he's needed. Remind him that you hold a special spot for him that's always vacant that only he can fill in your family.

Let Dads and Sons Develop Their Own Relationships

We moms spend the early years of our children's lives consumed with loving, nurturing, feeding, cleaning, protecting, providing, and training our children. As they grow older, we struggle to let them go, to become independent of us, to not need us. It's hard. Because of our strong instinctive "mother nature," at times it's even hard to trust our husbands with our boys.

I've talked with several friends who really struggle with this. One friend in particular has a husband who's like a big kid. She's afraid he won't watch their children carefully enough when she's gone. And he doesn't. But usually the kids are fine. He loves their children, and his playfulness adds a fun dimension to their lives. She's learned to leave them without fear and embrace her husband's carefree spirit.

Another friend, whose son is now out of college and lives independently, shared with me how hard it was for her to let her husband and son have their own relationship—especially because they fought so much. Recently her husband went alone to visit their son. During the trip her son called her and complained about Dad, how difficult he was being and how hard he was to be with. She responded, "You and your dad need to work things out with each other. I'm not there, and I'm not going to get involved." She didn't, even though she was tempted to call her husband and tell him how their son was feeling. She's disappointed that the two men in her life aren't as close as she had hoped, but she also feels a sense of freedom when she lets go of trying to fix their relationship and lets the two of them develop a relationship of their own.

God Is In Control

Abraham is a classic example in the Bible of a person giving up his son and trusting God to provide, to ultimately be the one in control.

God said, "Take your son, your only son, Isaac, whom you love, and go to the region of Moriah. Sacrifice him there as a burnt offering on one of the mountains I will tell you about." Early the next morning Abraham got up and saddled his donkey. He took with him two of his servants and his son Isaac. When he had cut enough wood for the burnt offering, he set out for the place God had told him about *(Genesis 22:2-3)*.

I don't believe God ever intended Abraham to kill Isaac. Child sacrifice doesn't fit with God's nature. I think God wanted Abraham to loosen his grip on Isaac and to see that He would take care of his most precious possession. I also think Abraham had enough faith in God to believe He would provide. And God did provide—at the last moment possible, but He *did* provide.

When I read this story, I'm reminded to trust God with my boys, but I also find myself wondering about Sarah, Abraham's wife. Where in the world was she during all of this? Did she trust Abraham as he walked off with a donkey, a knife, firewood, and Isaac, her only son? Or did someone have to hold her back as she kicked and screamed and watched Abraham and Isaac leave? I think that's what I would have been doing.

I don't know; I can only imagine.

I prefer to imagine Sarah trusting Abraham with Isaac. I like to think she knew the deep love Abraham had for Isaac, and she trusted he wouldn't let any harm befall their son. I also like to believe she knew Abraham's unfailing love for God and trusted him to be obedient to God in all things. God taught Abraham and Sarah an incredible lesson in letting go of their son and trusting God most of all, a lesson that's been passed down through generations and will continue to teach people about God's faithfulness.

Letting go of control is a lifelong struggle for many women. But letting go and clinging to trust leads to peace. "Cast all your anxiety on him because he cares for you" (1 Peter 5:7). And he cares for your boys. Trust most in God who loves you and loves your husband—and your boys— more than you can imagine.

Digging Deeper

My father used to play with my brother and me in the yard. Mother would come out and say, "You're tearing up the grass."

"We're not raising grass," Dad would reply. *"We're raising boys."*
—Harmon Killebrew, former major league baseball player
and member of the Hall of Fame.

Do you trust your husband with your boys? If not, why not? What steps can you take to let go and trust him more?

If your husband travels or works long hours, what specific steps can you take to make him feel needed at home when he's home?

Write a prayer to God asking Him to help you let go of control and learn to trust Him more.

Recommended Reading

Some other Bible verses encouraging trust in God: Jeremiah 29:11; Psalm 100:5; Proverbs 3:5-6; John 14:1-2; Philippians 4:6-7; Hebrews 11:17-19.

16. Like Father, Like Son

Train a child in the way he should go,
and when he is old he will not turn from it.
—Proverbs 22:6

Dave Meurer writes in his book *Boyhood Daze* about the male gender: "I GUARANTEE you that I know which gender will gleefully show their sons how to mash their faces against the Xerox machine to make copies of humorous facial expressions. And this particular gender would very likely do this for hours were it not for the fact that the glass gets hot and it starts to burn your skin."[1]

I'm not sure many moms would even dream of doing that with a copy machine.

He also advocates eating ice cream for breakfast and making decisions based on only two factors:

Is this expressly forbidden in either the Bible or the Code of Federal Regulations?

Would it be fun?[2]

Again, these would not be the first two factors a mom

would base her decisions on. However, I wouldn't mind eating ice cream for breakfast, especially with hot fudge topping. True enough, a mom can't teach a boy the things a dad can. Moms don't shave their faces, don't have the urge to wrestle, don't desire to copy their faces on a photocopier, and rarely find it tempting to throw firecrackers into a toilet. Most men really like all those things. Men have a special relationship with sons and a special understanding of what it's like to be a boy. Fathers need to take advantage of that knowledge and raise their boys with their unique gifts, ideas, convictions, and maleness.

Dads, you make a huge difference in the lives of your sons. Boys need men to model what it is to live as a good man. They need to share not just the quest for fun but also the more serious aspects of life, such as living with integrity, finding purpose, finding a job, choosing a wife, parenting children, handling disappointment, giving generously, believing in God, dealing with testosterone, and other important matters.

I asked the same men I asked in the previous chapter about how their moms impacted their lives about the impact their fathers had on who they are today. Here are some of their responses:

We talked about everything; no problem was too big for my dad.

He loved college football. He took me to all the Notre Dame games.

He told me, "People don't see the 95 percent of a job you do, but the 5 percent you did not finish." This encouraged me always to finish what I begin.

My dad was always there, even at my junior high basketball practices.

He frequently told me he was proud of me.

He exhibited a tremendous work ethic.

My dad was a passionate person. I remember him crying during family prayer times or when singing worship songs.

He encouraged me to ask questions and be open to other people and their ideas.

He went to court with me when I got my first speeding ticket.

He took me on a mission trip to Mexico, and we built a house for a family.

My dad was always honest. He never lied.

He treated my mom like a queen. He loved her with his life. When she died, he died shortly after.

Based on these responses, I outlined a few areas where fathers have a unique impact on their sons. Remember that this is an incomplete list. The influence a dad has on his son is so valuable that many good books are dedicated to this topic. Don't believe for a minute that you don't matter. You do.

Dads show boys how to be men. To become a man, a boy needs to see a man, to see how a man lives, works, plays, worships, and interacts with others. John Eldridge writes in his book *Wild at Heart*, "A boy learns who he is and what he's got from a man, or the company of men. He cannot learn it from other boys, and he cannot learn it from the world of women."[3]

Because men and women are different, and a boy knows he's a boy, he wants to learn from you, Dad, whether he admits it or not. And he'll model your behavior, good or bad.

It's all part of being a parent, perhaps the scariest part. A pastor once told Zane and me that when we married it was an opportunity to become more Christlike. We would have to become less selfish and more concerned about someone else. Then, when we had children, it would be another opportunity to become even more Christlike. This offered another time of growth, to give more of ourselves as we serve and raise our children. So the influence you have on your sons can be a motivation in your own life to live the way you really want to live so your son will live that way too. Your boys are watching you, and they'll do what you do.

Zane realized this early on, when Josh was probably two years old. Zane had reached into the refrigerator to grab the milk, and it slipped out of his hand. The cap flew off, and milk dribbled down into every little crack of the refrigerator, including the fruit and vegetable drawers. He's not one to curse frequently, but an unsavory word slipped out.

Josh was standing behind him holding his blue sippy-cup, waiting for some milk. As Zane grabbed a towel, he heard Josh's sweet little voice innocently utter that same word with the same inflection. Zane was mortified. He looked at Josh, who smiled, proud that he had learned a new word. That moment was etched in Zane's mind, and he knew that Josh—and our future kids—would imitate him. This experience motivated Zane to attempt to live a life worthy of imitating.

Remember—other men can also play a role in helping your boys grow into loving, respectable, responsible men. When our older two boys, Josh and Jordan, turned 13, Zane and several other men wrote them letters, sort of coming-of-age letters. They wrote phenomenal, life-impacting words of wisdom, encouraging them as men to be men. We laminated these and keep them in a safe place. I think these letters are something the boys will look back on at different times in their lives and find direction and encouragement from these men's wise words.

In fact, when I wrote this chapter, I had taken these letters out of the drawer to read. Josh found me in the family room and asked, "Mom, my letters are gone. Do you know where they are?" He had noticed something very important to him was gone, and he didn't want to lose these precious words of encouragement. I replaced them immediately, glad to know he had looked for them.

Dads instill courage. Dad's influence helps boys face the world with courage. Courage is defined by Dictionary.com as "the quality of mind or spirit that enables a person to face difficulty, danger, pain, etc., without fear; bravery."

Remember British 400-meter Olympic runner Derek Redman? He qualified for the 1992 Summer Olympics in Barcelona, Spain, after suffering a terrible injury that kept him out of the 1988 Olympics. After enduring 22 surgeries, he achieved his goal of competing in the 1992 Olympics. No one had thought he would compete at that level again, but he did.

When the gun fired, Derek took off, racing against the fastest men in the world. He was in the middle of the pack when he pulled his hamstring and fell to the ground. The broadcasters started yelling, "Redman is out of the race!" But Derek pulled himself up, determined to finish. Writhing in pain, with tears rolling down his cheeks, he slowly inched his way toward the finish line. He kept stumbling, and it didn't look as if he would make it.

Just as Redman was about to collapse for the final time, a man came running out of the stands. He climbed the fence, pushed his way past security guards, and ran onto the track. It was Jim Redman, Derek's dad. Jim put his hand on Derek's shoulder, and Derek fell into his chest. You could see his dad say something into his ear. He took Derek's arm and wrapped it around his shoulder, and then Jim put his arm around Derek and held him up. The crowd roared as Derek finished the race with his dad, arm in arm.

Later it was reported that what his dad said was "Derek, we started this thing together, and we're going to finish together."

That's the power of a father. Sometimes boys will experience success, other times failure, but knowing their dad supports them gives them the courage to go after their dreams—never to give up. Whatever your boys are going through, let them know you'll be with them from start to finish.

Dads keep boys out of jail—except in a vicious game of Monopoly. The good news is that boys with involved, emotionally close fathers are much less likely to be thrown into jail than boys who are reared without a dad. James Dobson writes in *Bringing Up Boys*, "Prisons are populated primarily by men who were abandoned or rejected by their fathers. Motivational speaker and writer Zig Ziglar quotes his friend Bill Glass, a dedicated evangelist who counseled almost every weekend for 25 years with men who were incarcerated, as saying that among the thousands of prisoners he had met, not one of them genuinely loved his dad."[4] When a boy has a good relationship with his father, he's probably less likely to get into serious trouble.

However, when it comes to Monopoly, at least in our household, if boys land in jail, they find no mercy from Zane. I usually cave in to their pleas for leniency.

I think our boys have a healthy fear and respect for Zane. Providing a firm voice, he's a man who does what he says, who doesn't falter in conviction, and who upholds boundaries for our boys. It's clear what lines they cannot cross, and if they do cross them, they'll be disciplined. I'm not as good at that as Zane is. I believe God put Zane and me together, a blend of tough and tender, to bring a healthy, well-rounded home experience to our boys. I know there are no guarantees on how our boys will end up. Their futures will be determined by the choices they make in life. But I'm thankful to have a partner who's strong where I'm weak and who shares the same ideals and hopes I share for the future of our sons.

Dads show boys how to treat girls. How Mom and Dad treat each other leaves a lasting imprint on their children. The marriage relationship children observe at home sets the standard in their minds for how marriages should operate. How you treat your wife is probably how your son will treat his future wife.

Treating women with love and respect begins at home, a place where you have influence. Outside the home, however, is a different battleground. Our culture regularly exploits women as objects and sex symbols, but I believe a father's influence is greater than any media blitz. You can instill in boys the need to treat women with respect as you encounter situations outside the home that do the opposite.

For example, it seems several movies that have been released recently have a villain who is female. I don't have a problem with this, but I do have a problem when the hero, usually a male in the movie, defeats the female villain in a brutal brawl.

My stomach churns as I watch a man beat up and kill a woman, even if she's evil. Most women are physically weaker than most men. That's a fact. With the rise of physical and sexual assault on women today, I think it's a very unhealthy trend to portray women in movies as physically strong as men and capable of fighting to the death against a man. Take opportunities to discuss this with your boys when the opportunity arises. I implore you to drill into your boys that it's wrong to ever hit or sexually assault a girl. That's one of my soapboxes. I believe men can make a difference in our world through training their sons to respect women and to defend women against such actions.

Dads affect how boys view God. I called a friend of mine who's a Christian counselor and asked her if she thinks a boy's relationship with his dad affects how he perceives God. She said yes, and added that most psychologists, counselors, psychiatrists, and pastors have found that to be true. She emphasized that this is the case not just for boys but for girls too. She also mentioned she spends a lot of time with her clients convincing them that their Heavenly Father is different than their earthly father. This makes perfect sense, because we refer to God as "God the Father." If a child has a father who's abusive, domineering, inattentive, and unconcerned with his life, that's how he'll see God. On the other hand, if a child has a father who's truthful, forgiving, attentive, and cares about even the tiniest aspects of his life, that's how he'll see God.

I know that's a big burden to carry, because no one is perfect, and we all make mistakes. But that's one of the responsibilities you inherited when you chose to become a dad. However, always remember 1 Peter 4:8: "Above all, love each other deeply, because love covers over a multitude of sins."

One of my all-time favorite comic strips is Bill Watterson's *Calvin and Hobbes*, featuring a six-year-old boy and his stuffed tiger. If you have boys, you can totally relate to Watterson's sense of humor and Calvin's very boyish, rambunctious persona. In one cartoon Calvin quizzes his dad about clouds: "What are clouds made of?" and "So how come they float?" His dad can't answer Calvin's questions, so Calvin concludes, "I take it there's no qualifying exam to be a dad."[5]

Anyone can become a dad. It's not necessary to study or pass a test to assume one of the most influential positions in life—a dad. Fortunately, the Bible, other men, and a wealth of resources can guide you on your adventure through fatherhood.

The journey is long and hard yet exhilarating and rewarding. Being a father gives you a purpose for living a passionate, honorable, fulfilling life. Leading young boys into unknown territory and helping them conquer fear, find their own purpose, experience their own adventures, pursue God, and grow up to be men who make the world a better place is not a job for the faint of heart. Be strong and courageous. Seek God with all your heart, and He will guide you as you guide the boys who follow in your footsteps.

Digging Deeper

*We all have different desires and needs, but if we don't discover
what we want from ourselves and what we stand for,
we will live passively and unfulfilled.*
—Bill Watterson.

Do you agree with the quote above? Why or why not?

Do you know what you stand for? Have you ever discussed this with your son? If not, read him the quote above and have a talk about what's worth living for.

Of the topics listed in this chapter about the different areas in which you have an influence in your son's life, which do you feel you do well with? Which do you feel you need to work on?

In what other areas do you feel you have an influence in your son's life?

Recommended Reading

Stark Raving Dad! by Dave Meurer

Better Dads, Stronger Sons: How Fathers Can Guide Boys to Become Men of Character, by Rick Johnson

Scriptures to read: Psalm 127:4-5; Proverbs 13:22; Matthew 18:6; Galatians 6:2; Ephesians 6:4; Colossians 3:21; Colossians 4:2.

17. Our Father Who Does Art in Heaven

The word of God is living and active. Sharper than any double-edged sword, it penetrates even to dividing soul and spirit, joints and marrow; it judges the thoughts and attitudes of the heart.
—Hebrews 4:12

I grew up going to church every Sunday. It was pretty boring. Sometimes my parents asked me where I wanted to sit. I always pointed to a seat close to a stained glass window on the right-hand side of the church. I think my parents thought I liked how the light filtered through the different colored glass, or that I liked the scene depicted on that particular window. But the real reason I liked that spot was that a spider had spun a web down in the corner, and I liked watching the flies get tangled in it and try to get free from the spider's grasp. This kept me entertained during the entire service.

—Tim, age 44

It's good to teach boys to sit quietly through a Sunday church service, but if it's possible to make learning about God fun, then why not?

Young Life founder Jim Rayburn says, "It's a sin to bore kids with the gospel." Really. Think about it. The Bible is filled with romance, betrayal, murder, miracles, war, and redemptive love, all the aspects of a bestselling novel and more. It is, in fact, the bestselling book of all time. According to Wikipedia, the approximate sales of the Bible to date are four to six billion. This is followed by the *Quotations of Chairman Mao* at 900 million, not even a close second. And the Bible has been made into numerous major motion pictures. Adding to all that the supernatural aspect of reading God's Word and the power it has to literally change lives, how do we manage to make it so boring?

Boys are doers. This was confirmed to me when a mom of boys sent me the following anonymous e-mail that was making the rounds, Internet proof that boys have the tendency to do just about anything if it involves action, good or bad:

Interesting things you discover when you have sons:

1. A king-size waterbed holds enough water to flood a 2,000-square-foot house four inches deep.

2. If you spray hair spray on dust bunnies and run over them with roller blades, they can ignite.

3. A three-year-old boy's voice is louder than 200 adults in a crowded restaurant.

4. If you hook a dog leash over a ceiling fan, you'll find the motor is not strong enough to rotate a 42-pound boy wearing Batman underwear and a Superman cape. It is strong enough, however, if a paint can is tied to it, to spread paint on all four walls of a 20 x 20-ft. room.

5. You should not throw baseballs up when the ceiling fan is on. When using a ceiling fan as a bat, you have to throw the ball up a few times before you get a hit. A ceiling fan can hit a baseball a long way.

6. *The glass in windows—even double-pane—doesn't stop a baseball hit by a ceiling fan.*

7. *When you hear the toilet flush and the words "Uh oh," it's already too late.*

8. *Brake fluid mixed with Clorox makes smoke, and lots of it.*

9. *A six-year-old boy can start a fire with a flint rock even though a 36-year-old man says they can do it only in the movies.*

10. *Certain Legos will pass through the digestive tract of a four-year-old boy.*

11. *"Play-Doh" and "microwave" should not be used in the same sentence.*

12. *Super Glue is forever.*

13. *No matter how much Jell-O you put in a swimming pool, you still can't walk on water.*

14. *Pool filters do not like Jell-O.*

15. *Garbage bags do not make good parachutes.*

16. *Marbles in gas tanks make lots of noise when the vehicle is being driven.*

17. *You probably DO NOT want to know what that odor is.*

18. *Always look in the oven before you turn it on; plastic toys do not like ovens.*

19. *The fire department in Austin, Texas, has a five-minute response time.*

20. *The spin cycle on the washing machine does not make earthworms dizzy.*

21. It will, however, make cats dizzy.

22. Cats throw up twice their body weight when dizzy.

23. Eighty percent of women will pass this on to almost all their friends, with or without kids.

24. Eighty percent of men who read this will try mixing the Clorox and brake fluid. (See #8 if you skipped ahead.)

Even when it comes to spiritual matters, boys are doer-oriented. For example, I determined to teach my boys The Lord's Prayer. I think we had just watched a football movie where the players, sitting and kneeling in a circle, recited it before a big game. I grew up in an Episcopal church where we said this prayer faithfully every week. Now we attend a nondenominational church that doesn't do that, so this movie scene encouraged me to have my boys memorize this essential prayer.

I wrote it down on a piece of paper and put it next to the boys' beds. Each night we said it together. Finally, when I thought they had learned it, I asked Jake to say it for me.

"Our Father, who does art in heaven," he began.

"Stop, that's not it," I said. "It's 'Our Father which art in heaven,' not 'who *does* art in heaven.'"

"But that doesn't make sense," he said.

"Why not?"

"It has to be 'Our Father who does art in heaven,' because that's what He does, right?"

"No, not exactly. 'Art in heaven' means he lives in heaven."

"Oh, I thought he did art like the sunrises and sunsets, stuff like that," he explained.

"Hmmm, well, I guess you're right. He does do lots of art in heaven," I admitted, admiring that train of thought.

This naturally led to Jake's asking, "Hey—what will we do all day when we get to heaven, anyway?" For Jake it's all about the doing.

Yet again, I gave my favorite answer to most of my boys' questions: "I have no idea."

We talked and wondered together about heaven. I told Jake I do know that heaven won't be boring and that God has created an amazing place for us to live eternally. Then I said, "I think we'll probably be able to do all our favorite things that we do on earth, but it will be way cooler and more fun than we can imagine."

To Jake, that meant skiing fresh tracks all day, doing tricks off humongous jumps without getting hurt, eating all the candy he wanted and never having to brush his teeth. It's fun to imagine and to hear what kids have to say.

Just like school, one of the best ways for boys to learn about God is to make it an active experience. Setting your boys down around the kitchen table, reading a Bible verse, and then lecturing them for 10 minutes on what this verse means is not going to grab and keep their attention. (Not that we've ever done this.)

Here's an alternative idea a friend gave me for an interactive Bible lesson perfect for boys. He bought little tubes of toothpaste for each family member. He then had them squeeze out all of the toothpaste onto the table. After they had done that, he asked them to put the toothpaste back into the tube. Of course, that was impossible. He then read the Bible verse Proverbs 21:23—"He who guards his mouth and his tongue keeps himself from calamity." He made the point that it's easy to say hurtful things to others, just as it's easy to squeeze out the toothpaste. But it's difficult to take back those words once they've escaped from your mouth, just as it was impossible to put the toothpaste back into the tube. Now that's a messy but brilliant lesson.

To gather more ideas for parents to teach boys about God, I called a friend, Scott Downing, who has worked with youth for 18 years through Young Life and now is a children's pastor at a local church. He suggested finger painting with younger boys.

"While painting the picture together, you can talk about creation. Then you can wipe the paint off your fingers on your shirt and talk about sin, and how it makes us unclean. Then you can take your shirt to the washing machine and clean it and talk about forgiveness and how God, through Jesus, made us clean."

Wow—he just spontaneously came up with that while we were on the phone! Not everyone is as creative as Scott, but everyone has the capacity to try.

Youth groups can be fun, if you can get your boys to go. We, however, have had a hard time getting our boys involved in one. Because of sports, homework, lack of friends willing to go, and all sorts of other reasons, it's been difficult. I wish with all my heart they desired to go, but they don't. So we've had to try harder to teach them about God at home. I guess that's been a good thing. Instead of relying on someone else to train our boys, we've embraced that responsibility.

I mentioned this challenge to Scott, and he had some suggestions for encouraging spiritual growth for middle school- and high school-age boys, such as using movies to teach lessons. A Web site he recommends is <www.screen vue.com>. It has 3,000 clips to choose from. Boys are doers, and they are visual, so they enjoy a good movie clip followed with thought-provoking questions, which are also included on the Web site. Scott said he's found this activity can lead to great discussions.

Storytelling is another method Scott suggested to make God's Word come alive. Most people love a good story, and as I mentioned in a previous chapter, stories stick in your mind and help make spiritual points memorable. Remember: Jesus was a master storyteller.

Scott said he learned through his training with Young Life that when teaching a Bible lesson, you should add some imagery to it to make it more powerful. Fill in the gaps. For example, if he's teaching about the disciples in a boat, he'll paint a picture with words about the rocking of the boat, the waves splashing over the sides and soaking their feet. He'll describe the disciples' frantic efforts to get the water out of the boat. Then he can try to help the kids imagine the fear the disciples felt because the storm was so severe they felt they might die.

He uses phrases such as "I wonder if . . ." or "I imagine that . . ." Or he'll ask his audience, "How would you feel if . . . ?" He's found that these phrases and questions, along with using storytelling techniques, grab boys' attention and pulls them into the scene.

"It's a creative method of making the story relevant to their lives," Scott explained.

I think another idea is to literally put your family's faith in action. Be doers together. Build a house for Habitat for

Humanity together. Make cookies for neighbors. Invite missionaries to stay with you. Adopt a child through an organization like Compassion. Buy a bagel and give it to a homeless person. The Bible says God's Word is "living and active . . . Sharper than any double-edged sword" (Hebrews 4:12). So it shouldn't be too hard to keep it living and active in our boys' lives. Be creative—just don't be boring.

Prayer Is Like Air

I not only want the boys to know God—I also want them to pray and talk to God as naturally as they brush their teeth. Correction—let me use another example, because they don't like to brush their teeth. Let's say as naturally as they leave dirty socks lying all around the house and the backyard. Truly, I want my boys to pray as easily as they breathe. I believe in the power of prayer. I've experienced the power of prayer. I want my boys to know it too.

So I asked Scott for some ideas on how to encourage boys to pray. He emphasized the best way to teach boys to talk to God is to model it for them. Talking to God doesn't have to be right before a meal or bed. And talking to God doesn't mean you have to stop life. You can talk to God anywhere, anytime. Parents can show this to their boys through saying short, spontaneous, middle-of-a-moment, random prayers.

"Let's say you're eating a really good strawberry," Scott explained. "And you say in front of your son, 'Wow—this is an awesome strawberry. It tastes great.' Then you might add, 'Thank you, God, for making this strawberry.' If you do that constantly, you're showing your son how to talk to God all the time."

As I thought about this, I realized Zane and I do that sometimes when we pass an accident while driving. We'll say a prayer out loud for the people involved. Not long ago we passed a bad accident, and Jake suggested we pray for those people. So I know it's becoming a part of their nature. I continue to pray for my boys to experience how God works through our prayers and to learn to pray continually.

Finding Quiet in the Noise

I love what Oswald Chambers encourages: "We have to pitch our tents where we shall always have quiet times with God, however noisy our times with the world may be."[1] I don't know about you, but I suspect that if you're reading this book, then your world is noisy like mine is. Finding quiet in the midst of chaos is challenging. Living in a loud house, full of the noise of boys, doesn't lend itself to long hours of quiet reflection. But I'm okay with that. My tent is pitched in the middle of a noisy life, a life I love.

Yet I do manage to occasionally find some sweet, calm times alone with God. Usually it's in the morning before anyone else wakes up. Not every day, but if I make the effort, I usually find God is already there waiting for me. I find that if I don't make an effort to grow in my relationship with God, then I run out of what it takes to encourage others, especially my boys.

Getting to know God and sharing that experience with my boys in a creative, interactive, playful, energetic manner can be an adventure, like mixing brake fluid and Clorox. A reaction can take place that excites the hearts of boys, causing them to want to know more, to do more, and eventually to have their own understanding and relationship with the God—who does art in heaven.

Digging Deeper

Some things boys said about what heaven will be like:

"Clouds you play on and everyone's nice."

"You'll have a beautiful house."

"Blue clouds, and once you look down, everything you see is toys and Legos."

"Big cloud with a really cool man, like 2,000 feet wide."

"It's made out of donuts."

What do you think heaven will be like? Ask your boys this question too.

Be creative and come up with an idea for a Bible lesson for your boys that involves making a mess. Then do it.

How do you find a quiet place for yourself in a house full of noise?

Recommended Reading

Intimate Moments, by Ken Gire.

Here are other Bible verses on teaching your children about God: Deuteronomy 6:5-8; Psalm 78:1-4; Psalm 145:3-13; Matthew 6:5-13; 1 John 5:14-15.

18. Life's a Game—
Have a Ball!

Never be lacking in zeal, but keep your spiritual fervor, serving the Lord.
Be joyful in hope, patient in affliction, faithful in prayer.
—Roman 12:11-12

Boys love games. Whether it's basketball, Risk, or a contest to see who can hit the street sign out front with the tennis ball, games are fun.

Sometimes it's difficult, and not always responsible, to view life as a game, especially when some hard, not-so-fun stuff happens. But if you strive to keep a playful attitude in your heart and mind most of the time, then life will be easier for you to enjoy—to have a ball with your boys.

As parents of boys, we're in danger of getting stuck in ruts of fear, control, misunderstanding, and other negative traits. We can spend sleepless nights worrying about the decisions our boys make or will make. We can try to manipulate their circumstances to give them what we feel are important prospects in life. We can argue with them until we're blue in the face about why they need to learn Spanish and do their math homework.

We can also get caught up in training and disciplining our boys, focusing on who they'll become rather than enjoying who they are today. We can hire professional athletes to physically train our boys. We can sign them up for test preparation classes, music lessons, and all sorts of learning opportunities. We do our best to ensure our boys become great at whatever they do. Giving our boys the best is admirable, but this can consume us. We can find ourselves living in the future, not in the now.

"Life is what happens to you while you're busy making other plans," John Lennon said. This is profoundly true. We can become so engrossed in making plans for our boys that we miss the opportunity to just do life with them. Planning is important, but we can make the mistake of focusing on the planning and missing out on the everyday experiences that build relationship with our boys. We forget to have fun during the game, because we focus on the end result.

Carol Kuykendall writes, "'Make the most of life's irretrievable moments,' someone older and wiser told me. Since then, those seven simple words have helped me make choices about what matters most."[1] These seven words can help all of us make choices, every day.

Ask yourself throughout your day, "What's happening now that might not happen again?" Are your boys outside building a snow fort and planning a huge snowball fight while you're cleaning the garage or fixing the washer? Maybe you should put down that broom or screwdriver and go outside and play. The disorganized garage and broken washer aren't going anywhere. They'll still be there in an hour or so.

Choose to get in the game with your boys, and be in the game. We can easily become distracted from what's important—growing healthy, happy boys who love God and love others.

That's what boy-sterous living is really all about—living a day-to-day life with passion, adventure, a sense of humor, and endless energy.

I pray God blesses you on your journey of raising your boys. May you be full of godly zeal, joy, hope, and patience, and be faithful to pray always.

Thank God for the noise of boys reminding you to live life to the fullest. Live loud, and love lots!

Bloopers

I love watching bloopers at the end of movies. They're funny and so real. Seeing the actors and actresses mess up and crack up is pure entertainment. So for those of you who read to the very last page, I decided to put some parenting bloopers at the back of this book.

This is a reminder that no parents are perfect. No families are perfect. We've all made mistakes with our boys. Below are some of the stories parents shared with me about the mistakes they've made. All the stories are true; however, the names have been changed to protect the guilty.

Blooper #1: "J" Is for Jelly

One morning Jill's year-old son was screaming his lungs out because he woke up hungry. She stuck him in his highchair and went to the fridge to get a jar of baby food. To her horror, they were completely out. His pitiful screaming made her desperate to find a quick way to curb his hunger pains. Then she saw the jar of grape jelly. The label claimed "mostly fruit." *Perfect!* she thought.

She unscrewed the lid, took his little baby spoon, and started feeding him the jelly straight from the jar. Like a baby bird, he kept opening his mouth, swallowing the jelly, and opening his mouth for another bite. Her husband walked into the kitchen and saw what she was feeding their little guy.

"I don't think he should eat that," he said. "It's mostly sugar; he'll probably puke."

"Oh, no—look at him. He loves it. He'll be fine."

Suddenly the baby's stomach grumbled. He made some gurgling noises and promptly threw up the jar of jelly. Purple liquid filled the high-chair tray. He's now a teenager and still won't touch jelly.

Blooper #2: The Butcher's Shop of Horror

Lisa and her husband had ordered a portion of a cow in order to stock up on meat. The butcher called and told her that her order was ready. The store was near her home, and she decided it would be a good educational outing for Tyler, her three-year-old son. They went inside the shop, and the butcher asked if he would like to see what they do. He nodded his head.

"Come on back here," the butcher said.

Lisa and Tyler walked behind the counter to an oversized door. The butcher opened the door, and the moment Lisa saw what was inside, she knew this was a very, very bad idea. Hanging on giant meat hooks from the ceiling were dozens of fresh cow carcasses. The floor was covered with blood. She looked at Tyler, whose eyes were wide open. He had a look of sheer terror on his face. He covered his eyes with his chubby hands, and she quickly slammed the door shut.

After paying for her order, she put Tyler into the car and left as fast as possible. On the way home Tyler said, "Mommy, my eyes shouldn't have seen that."

Blooper #3: Sweet Dreams

One afternoon Leslie couldn't get Mitchell, her 18-month-old, to fall asleep for his nap. They had just had lunch, and she had given him a little chocolate chip cookie from a box, and now he wanted more. She told him, "No more, sweetie," and put him in his crib. He cried and cried. Every time she checked on him, he was standing up, his cheeks wet from tears, his arms stretched out reaching for her and for another cookie.

"Cookie, cookie," he pleaded.

She was exhausted. Her newborn was sleeping, and she wanted to take a nap too. She tried everything from rocking him to playing music, but nothing kept him quiet. Finally she gave in and handed him the entire box of cookies.

About an hour later a friend came over. Because Leslie was busy nursing the baby, she asked her friend to check on Mitchell. Her friend opened the door, and Mitchell sat in his crib with chocolate smeared around his lips, on his pj's, on the sheets and the walls—well, just about everywhere. He was playing with an empty box. She picked him up, along with the box, and brought him to Leslie. "I don't think you're supposed to give him this," she mentioned, balancing Mitchell on her hip with one hand and holding the empty box in the other.

Embarrassed, Leslie explained how she desperately needed sleep. It took several days of Mitchell crying himself to sleep before he realized he wouldn't get a box of cookies in his crib every day for naptime.

Blooper #4: Through the Fire

Terry saw the dark line of smoke snaking up into the blue sky. Then she heard the fire trucks. *I bet Daniel would love to see the fire trucks up close and in action,* she thought. She scooped her two-year-old up and into the car in search of the fire. She drove in the direction of the smoke until she could hear the alarms. Excited for her son to experience a real fire, she rolled down the windows and slowly drove down the street where a fire truck had just turned.

A house was on fire, and the firemen were racing around, working to put it out. The truck alarms were blaring, and the fire was growing bigger by the minute. She parked across the street, assuming her son would find this fascinating. Instead, he started crying and yelling, "Hot! Hot!" She quickly rolled up the windows and drove away.

For the next couple weeks, every time she put Daniel into the car he would place his hands on the windows and say, "Hot." And for the next several months he wouldn't get anywhere near their BBQ grill.

Blooper #5: The Exterminator

Karen's son's hamster was on the brink of death. The boy's pet had been diagnosed with cancer a couple of days earlier and had not been given long to live. It was difficult watching him suffer, so she called the vet who told her it cost $100 to put the animal to sleep. *A hundred dollars?* she thought—*for a hamster? That's crazy.* She told her son to tell his pet good-bye before leaving for school, because the hamster probably wouldn't make it through the day. After her son left, she couldn't stand to watch the hamster suffer anymore. She decided she would help him along. She put the rodent in a plastic bag, attached it to the car exhaust pipe and turned on the car. After a few minutes the deed was done.

When her older son came home, she had to tell someone the truth. She assumed he was old enough not to tell his little brother the details. She assumed wrong.

When her younger son came home and found out his pet had died, he went to tell his older brother, who without a pause said, "He didn't die—Mom killed him."

Thank the Lord, love covers a multitude of mistakes!

Please send me your parenting bloopers: <jean@jean-blackmer.com>.

P.S. Don't worry. If they're published, I'll keep your identity a secret.

Notes

Chapter 1

1. David Meurer, *Good Spousekeeping* (Colorado Springs: Cook Communications, 2004), 87.

2. Carole Fawcett, "The Science of Laughter," <http://ezinearticles.com/?The-science-of-Laughter&id=61158>.

Chapter 3

1. Carol Kuykendall, *Five-Star Families: Moving Yours from Good to Great* (Grand Rapids: Revell, 2005), 92.

2. David Gurian, *The Wonder of Boys,* (New York: Tarcher/Putnam, 1997), 23.

3. Ibid., 23.

Chapter 4

1. Leonard Sax, *Boys Adrift: The Five Factors Driving the Growing Epidemic of Unmotivated Boys and Underachieving Young Men* (New York: Basic Books, 2007), 60.

2. Elinor Ochs, "The Multitasking Generation," *Time*, March 27, 2006, <http://www.time.com/time/magazine/article/0,9171,1174696-200.html>.

3. Tamar Lewin, "At Colleges, Women Are Leaving Men in the Dust," *New York Times,* July 9, 2006.

4. Sax, *Boys Adrift*, 59.

Chapter 5

1. Aron Ralston, *Between a Rock and a Hard Place* (New York: Atria Books, 2004), 113.

2. Luci Swindoll, *I Married Adventure: Looking at Life Through the Lens of Possibility* (Nashville: W Publishing Group, 2002), 82.

Chapter 6:

1. Bob Bigelow, Tom Moroney, and Linda Hall, *Just Let the Kids Play: How to Stop Other Adults from Ruining Your Child's Fun and Success in Youth Sports* (Deerfield Beach, Fla.: Health Communications, 2001), 50.

Chapter 7

1. Nurses' health study from Harvard Medical School <http://www.anapsid.org/cnd/gender/tendfend.html/>.

2. Laura Jensen Walker, *Girl Time: A Celebration of Chick Flicks, Bad Hair Days & Good Friends* (Grand Rapids: Revell, 2004), 10-11.

Chapter 8

1. *Advanced Data from Vital and Health Statistics*, table 2, 386 (June 29, 2007):12.

Chapter 9

1. Kitty Harmon, *Up to No Good: The Rascally Things Boys Do* (San Francisco: Chronicle Books, 2000), 86.

2. Tally Flint, *The Mommy Diaries: Finding Yourself in the Daily Adventure* (Grand Rapids: Revell, 2008), 51.

Chapter 11

1. Harmon, *Up to No Good*, 11.

2. Shaunti Feldhahn, *For Women Only: What You Need to Know About the Inner Lives of Men* (Sisters, Oreg.: Multnomah Publishers, 2004), 179-80.

Chapter 12

1. Oswald Chambers, *My Utmost for His Highest* (New York: Dodd, Mead & Company, 1935), 247.

2. <http://www.cbsnews.com/stories/2005/01/14/eveningnews/print able667174.shtml>.

Chapter 13

1. Harmon, *Up to No Good*, 32.

Chapter 14

1. John and Helen Burns, *What Dads Need to Know About Daughters/ What Moms Need to Know About Sons* (New York: Howard Books, 2007), 43.

2. James Dobson, *Bringing Up Boys: Practical Advice and Encouragement for Those Shaping the Next Generation of Men* (Wheaton, Ill.: Tyndale House Publishers, 2001), 85.

Chapter 16

1. Dave Meurer, *Boyhood Daze: An Incomplete Guide to Raising Boys* (Minneapolis: Bethany House Publishers, 1999), 132.

2. Ibid., 136.

3. John Eldredge, *Wild at Heart* (Nashville: Thomas Nelson, 2001), 62.

4. Dobson, *Bringing Up Boys*, 60.

5. Bill Watterson, *The Authoritative Calvin and Hobbes* (Kansas City: Universal Press Syndicate, 1990), 40.

Chapter 17

1. Chambers, *My Utmost for His Highest*, 6.

Chapter 18

1. Quoted in Elisa Morgan, Mom, You Make a Difference! Encouraging Reminders for Real Moms (Grand Rapids, Mich.: Revell Books, 2005), 71.

Also from Beacon Hill Press

From financial concerns to passing on macho, *Single Moms Raising Sons* offers honest insight, unifying encouragement, and practical applications to help mothers raise their boys to be the solid, Christian men they want them to be.

Single Moms Raising Sons
Preparing Boys to Be Men When There's No Man Around
By Dana S. Chisholm

ISBN: 978-0-8341-2308-3

Available wherever books are sold.

Make a Lasting Difference in Your Child's Life

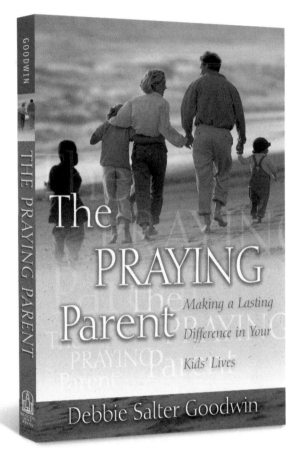

The most important gift you will ever give your child is prayer. This book provides scripture, illustrations, reflection questions, and specific examples to help you learn to pray for your children throughout the moments and stages of their lives.

The Praying Parent
By Debbie Salter Goodwin

ISBN: 978-0-8341-2176-8

Available wherever books are sold.

Where can you find the retreat you need?

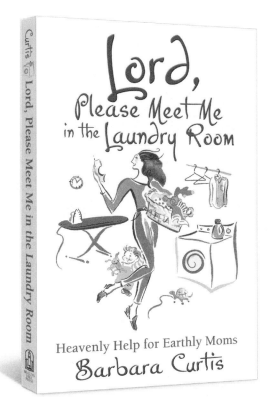

Lord, Please Meet Me in the Laundry Room brings ideas for spiritual retreats into the everyday life of busy moms. This book will unburden, enlighten, amuse, and encourage you in your hectic daily life.

Lord, Please Meet Me in the Laundry Room
By Barbara Curtis
ISBN-13: 978-0-8341-2097-6

BEACON HILL PRESS
OF KANSAS CITY

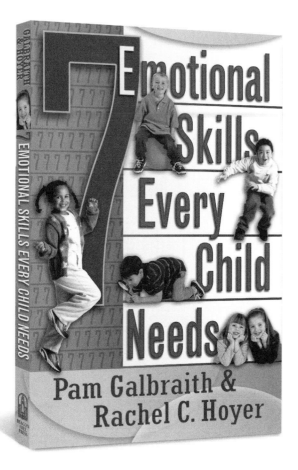

Also from Beacon Hill Press

Discover how you can help your child develop the emotional skills and traits that lead to healthy relationships with others and an authentic relationship with God.

7 Emotional Skills Every Child Needs
By Pam Galbraith and Rachel C. Hoyer

ISBN: 978-0-8341-2049-5

Available wherever books are sold.